The
Cultural
Evolution
Inside of
Mormonism

The
Cultural
Evolution
Inside of
Mormonism

by Greg Trimble

ISBN 13: 978-0692066188

Cover image © 2017 by Margie Clayton
Cover design and interior artwork by Leah McQueen
Cover design © 2017 by Greg Trimble
Copyedited by McKell Parsons and typeset by Deborah Spencer

To every member of the Church

Other Books by Greg Trimble

Dads Who Stay and Fight:
How to Be a Hero for Your Family

The Virtual Missionary: The
Power of Your Digital Testimony

Contents

Introduction

It's happening: a cultural evolution.

Over the last few years, I've had interactions with thousands of Mormons online through my blog. This book describes what I've seen. What I'm seeing. And what I hope to see more of in the future.

This book is an analysis of those observations as well as an attempt to understand some of the things that have presented the most significant stumbling blocks for my friends and family members over the last few years. My hope is that you'll read this book and then share it with someone who might need what is inside these pages.

In no way am I suggesting that my observations are prophetic. They are, in every definition of the word, just my "observations." These observations are honest, raw, and real, and they have given me great hope for the futurity of the Church and the ushering in of the Second Coming of Christ.

To the humble few: I'll see you in Zion.

More Extended Hands

"Inasmuch as ye have done it unto one of the least
of these my brethren, ye have done it unto me."
—*Jesus Christ (Matthew 25:40)*

At age 21, my life was made. I spent my days under the warm California sun, with the cool onshore ocean breeze and scent of salt water in the air. I played lots of baseball, surfed, and hung out with my friends. I wasn't going to church very often and I had just signed a full scholarship in Hawaii to finish my collegiate baseball career or to the minor leagues to take my shot at Major League Baseball. My life was filled with one fun adventure after another. From San Diego to LA, I had the coast covered, and I couldn't have dreamed up a better situation at age 21. There was just one issue though. After all was said and done for the day, I'd lay my head down on my pillow at night . . . and all I felt was emptiness. What the heck?

Exactly one night before my baseball season started, I was lying in bed, unable to fall asleep. During that night

I had a spiritual experience that would be hard for me to describe here in this book. What I can tell you, though, is that as a result of that experience, I learned that "you cannot do wrong and feel right."[1] I learned that "God will feel after you and he will take hold of you and wrench your very heart strings."[2] And most of all I learned that what Paul stated in Acts 17:27–29 is true, that I am a son of God, and that He is "not far from any one of us," especially when the nights are the darkest.

As a result of that experience, I decided I would try and go to church a couple of times. At that point, I was as raw and unpolished as they come. Can you believe I would go to Del Taco on Sunday and actually sneak burritos into church? I wasn't quite as bad as an Alma or a Paul in their heyday, but sometimes I look back at myself and wonder, "Who was that guy?"

It was hard for me to go to church. I didn't feel good about myself and I was friendless. No familiar faces among a sea of strangers. I went to the Newport Beach young single adult ward, didn't really talk to anyone, and left. Then I went to the Huntington Beach ward. But again, I didn't really talk to anyone and left. I don't really like to go into a room where I don't know anyone, but I knew I needed to be in church, and deep down I wanted to go on a mission. Going to sacrament meeting and then grabbing my surfboard just wasn't cutting it . . . so I decided I'd try to last the

---

1 Ezra Taft Benson, "A Message to the Rising Generation," *Ensign*, November 1977.
2 John Taylor, in *Journal of Discourses*, 1:24.

entire three hours! I still remember the first day I stayed for the whole block as if it were yesterday. I was sitting in third hour, wondering how I made it so long. No one had talked to me, and I thought I was too cool to reach out to anyone else. (Yeah . . . I was an idiot) I don't know what would have happened during the following week. I may have never come back . . . but out of the blue, a guy I had never seen before came and sat next to me.

"Hey, my name's Jevin," he said with a big grin on his face, extending his hand.

I hesitantly shook his hand and said, ". . . Hey man, I'm Greg."

Before I knew it, Jevin had me talking as if we were great buds. After the class was over, he casually asked, "Hey Greg, you want to grab some dinner with us?" Sounded good to me. It wasn't some Mormon "fellowship" obligation deal that ended with the last amen for the day. It was a genuine attempt to make a friend out of someone who looked really lonely. So we walked out into the foyer and he introduced me to about twenty people. The last person he introduced me to that day happened to be a girl . . . and she was a *ten*. (More to come on that later. . . .) I didn't realize it, but he was one of the coolest dudes in the ward. This guy didn't need any more friends, and he certainly didn't need to talk to me, but he went out of his way to do just that. Jevin's character enabled him to be an instrument in the hands of God on my behalf at that time. "Character is how you treat people that can do nothing for you."[3] There was absolutely nothing I could do for Jevin when he befriended me. Spencer W. Kimball once said that "God does notice us, and he watches over us. But it is usually through another person that he meets our needs."[4]

There is no way I could have known then just how significant this little tiny experience was with Jevin. When I look back on the events that transpired, I'm able to see it for the miracle that it is. This much I can tell you: Jevin probably didn't think twice about it, but I know that he was sent by God Himself to "watch over me" and to "meet my needs." He was eight or ten years my senior. He had no business sitting next to me and introducing himself to me that day. He was a returned missionary . . . and a cool one. I needed that. Within a few months I moved out of the "baseball house" and in with Jevin. I needed that. I met with the bishop and told him I wanted to go on a mission. He got me on the right track and challenged me to read the Book of Mormon. I needed that. The Book of Mormon, repentance, and prayer helped me feel the power of the Atonement. Like Alma, "I cried within my heart: O Jesus, thou Son of God, have mercy on me, who am in the gall of bitterness, and am encircled about by the everlasting chains of death. And now, behold, when I thought this, I could remember my pains no

---

3 Malcolm S. Forbes, *The Sayings of Chairman Malcolm* (New York: Harper & Row, 1978), 45.
4 Spencer W. Kimball, "Small Acts of Service," *Ensign*, December 1974.

more; yea, I was harrowed up by the memory of my sins no more." (Alma 36:18–19). Oh, how I needed that!

I prepared to serve a mission every day from that time forward. I was converted, and I wanted to share that conversion with others. I reached out to my best friend, Brian, with whom I'd never shared the gospel before. Never. We grew up in the same neighborhood and hung out almost every day of our lives. Mormonism didn't mean much to him because it didn't mean much to me. But after my own conversion, I shared zealously the gospel with him, and before I left on my mission, he was also converted and was baptized. I can still clearly remember our embrace as we stood there in our wet clothes in an Orange County baptismal font. Soon after his baptism, I left on a mission, and one year later, Brian himself sold his boat and left on a mission at age twenty-three. It wasn't easy for him to make such a decision, but as he'll tell you himself, that decision changed his life. Check out what Brian wrote me in an email while he was out on his mission:

```
Hey, I don't know if you remember but today is my 3 year mark of being baptized.
I have been a missionary longer than a member.Â  Thats wierd.Â  Oct 19th 2002 was
a sweet day.Â  1820 changed history, 2002 changed my history forever.
```

When Brian got home from his mission, he married an Idaho girl named Deneese. There is no possible way that this could have taken place if Brian hadn't joined the Church and gone on a mission. Their beautiful kids, Camden, Greyson, and Beckett, would never exist. Their family wouldn't be a family without this string of events. Generations inside and outside of his family would have been deprived of his testimony.

As for me and my family . . . do you remember that girl Jevin introduced me to that day in the foyer? Yeah, she's sitting next to me right now as I write this book. Before I left on my mission we were engaged. It's pretty rare to be engaged on a mission—and just as rare to have someone wait for over 2 years—but here we are.

"By small and simple means are great things brought to pass" (Alma 37:6). We need to forget fellowshipping and start friendshipping. This one small act of friendship—an extended hand, a smile, and a dinner invitation—changed my life, my family's life, my best friend's life, and the lives of thousands of other people to whom I was able to bear my testimony. It was the strengthening I needed at a pivotal time in my life, and its effects are endless. Imagine if Jevin didn't come up to me that day. I probably wouldn't have my wife and kids. I might have not followed through and served a mission. My best friend Brian wouldn't have joined the Church, served a mission, or married his wife. You would probably not be reading this book right now without that one interaction that took place in a church class long ago. I couldn't imagine my life without those things! I just can't.

This is what I want the world to know: all of what I just shared here might not have ever happened if this one random guy had not come up to me to extend his hand of friendship. It's almost as if the clasp of his hand held some sort of cosmic significance as I stood at a spiritual fork in the road. That moment in time was God's way of giving me an opportunity to live up to the potential and foreordination I had before I came to this earth.

So . . . next time you see someone sitting in church all alone, think of me and consider what it might mean to that person if you just extended your hand and offered your friendship.

Fewer Wrecking Balls

"I begin to speak only when I'm certain
what I'll say isn't better left unsaid."
—*Cato*[5]

Not too long ago, my wife and I were assigned to home and visit teach the same family in our ward. This family consisted of a very humble and genuine woman, her non-member husband, and an unbaptized nine-year-old daughter. The woman explained to us that she was born in the covenant as a member of the Church but stopped coming when she was a young woman. She described being picked on and gossiped about by some of the other young women in her ward. By now, this woman had been out of the Church for many years. Missionaries would go by their house but to no avail. By this point, she had established some habits that would wear on her conscience if she ever tried to return to church.

---

5 As quoted in Plutarch, *Cato the Younger*, chapter 4.

When we were assigned to teach this family, my wife was able to establish a relationship of trust and friendship with her. It took about three years of the most dedicated visiting teaching I have ever seen just to get this woman to be open to coming to a church event. Finally, after many years and at the request of my wife, this woman decided to bring her family to an activity. That led to this family attending church on Sunday, and attending church led to her daughter having a desire to be baptized.

But then there was that week when we weren't at church with them. Oh yes . . . that infamous Sunday when this woman and her husband attended a Gospel Principles class on their own. The woman smoked and drank, as did her husband. They didn't need anyone to tell them to feel guilty about those things. That was why they were at church in the first place. But sure enough, some insensitive soul in that class decided that it was their prerogative to censure people who break the Word of Wisdom. That was the last time anyone saw this family at church.

Now, I believe that those in the Church who find joy in "casting stones" are in the minority . . . but unfortunately their impact is felt by so many. Like giant demolition wrecking balls, they crush everyone who gets in their path and make church attendance an unbearable thought for too many tender souls. These insensitive members often mix up the difference between judging for yourself and actually judging others. Of course, judging for yourself between right and wrong is important. Of course, we're required to make daily, even minute-by-minute, judgments. But that doesn't mean we have the ability or right to judge and label others, especially when we rarely, if ever, have the whole picture. Our role in this life, as it pertains to others, is to give them the benefit of the doubt.

Why is it so hard for people to just be nice to each other? What is it about the Sermon on the Mount that even some stalwart members of the Church don't understand? What is unclear about the Savior's request to "judge not, that ye be not judged. For with what judgment ye judge, ye shall be judged" (Matthew 7:1–2)? What is it that keeps people from seeing the good in others, and why can't we just keep our thoughts to ourselves if they're not aimed to lift and bless? Why do so many people derive pleasure from trying to correct others' faults before they correct their own faults?

It's impossible to misunderstand the Savior's intent on what He's said about judging. Judging others IS. NOT. GOOD. In fact, the way you judge others will be the way you are judged in the hereafter. In reading the scriptures, I can come to no other conclusion than that Christ detested one thing above all else: judging, self-righteous, scheming, gossiping hypocrites. It just oozes from the pages. Especially from Matthew 23. It's the bold and the boisterous—as well as those who prefer to just whisper behind your back—who put the general membership of the Church on edge. Not the guy who is embarrassed to sit in the pew because he smells like smoke.

Both my wife and I have different friends who specifically stopped going to church in their younger years because they were made fun, left out, or picked on. One of these people has come back to church. The other still has a hard time coming back. But both of them believe with all their heart that the Church is true. It wasn't doctrine or history that's kept them at bay—it was a lack of feeling wanted and included.

In an even more recent Sunday School class, I witnessed a man publicly criticize a few sisters in the class whom he felt were not being doctrinally accurate. But as I quietly listened to the one-way exchange, as far as I could tell, he was the one who was doctrinally wrong, and these sisters appeared to be in harmony with the teachings of the modern prophets. Regardless of who was right or wrong, no one likes to be embarrassed in front of others . . . and maybe that's just enough to get someone to not want to attend that ward anymore. For better or worse, people remember the things you say, and they may never be able to forget. Wounds to the soul and psyche, unfortunately, can linger.

There will be those who read those last two paragraphs and say, "Well, those people just get offended too easily." I get it. I know there are many talks out there about not being offended and that people should choose to not be offended. But I'm tired of hearing that excuse by people who want to say whatever they want whenever they want. This doesn't give you a perpetual right to be offensive! Why can't we focus more on just being kind, instead of trying to put someone down for being offended? Everyone will eventually be offended, regardless of how thick their skin is. It's a human reaction to being degraded and threatened, and the result is a "fight or flight" response, neither of which is good for the Church or the individual.

Please don't take me wrong. I'm not saying that this is the norm. What I am saying is that when it does happen, it can alter lives and eternities . . . and all it takes is one experience to put someone down a thorny path.

These walking bulldozers of emotions usually manifest themselves in one of two ways. The loud and boisterous have no problem calling others out right in front of other people. They might give a biting or sarcastic remark that echoes in the cultural hall, or they might make a subtle jab at you during a Sunday school lesson. According to them, they're just "saying it like it is" or "calling it like they see it." They're just "speaking the truth" as they carve a path of spiritual destruction everywhere that they go.

On the other end of the spectrum, we've got another much subtler method of judging. This form of judging is done with whispers and epithets . . . and usually goes by the formal name of gossiping. It's carried out by people who are wholly insecure in their own skin and can find no other relief but by bringing others down and making them look bad. Have you ever been on the receiving end of a circle of gossipers? Have you ever had to go to a meeting or an event where you knew that people had been bad mouthing you behind your back? It's no fun. But to experience this pain at church, of all places. . . . As James says, "These things ought not so to be" (James 3:10).

Have you ever wondered why Alma gave up his judgment seat and entered into the ministry full time? It was because members of the Church couldn't figure out how to be kind to each other. Alma gave up his judgment seat for one major reason: he "saw and beheld with great sorrow that the people of the church began to be lifted up in the pride of their eyes . . . [and] that they began to be scornful, one towards another, and they began to persecute those who did not believe according to their own will and pleasure" (Alma 4:8).

"I often wonder why some feel they must be critical of others," said Elder Wirthlin. "It gets in their blood, I suppose, and it becomes so natural they often don't even think about it. They seem to criticize everyone—the way Sister Jones leads the music, the way Brother Smith teaches a lesson or plants his garden. Even when we think we are doing no harm by our critical remarks, consequences often follow. I am reminded of a boy who handed a donation envelope to his bishop and told him it was for him. The bishop, using this as a teaching moment, explained to the boy that he should mark on the donation slip whether it was for tithing, fast offerings, or for something else. The boy insisted the money was for the bishop himself. When the bishop asked why, the boy replied, 'Because my father says you're one of the poorest bishops we've ever had.'"[6]

An old Church News article revealed that "Some members fret over outside voices that try to destroy or discredit the Church. However, our greater concern probably lies with the 'wolves' who, wearing sheep's clothing, blend in

---

6 Joseph B. Wirthlin, "The Virtue of Kindness," *Ensign*, May 2005.

with the flock. 'Ravening' is an apt description of what they do: hungrily search for prey. The damage they do, not to the body of the Church but to individual souls, is immense. Other wolves in sheep's clothing, perhaps not fully grown, are also among us. They divide and scatter the flock, as it were, with such negative influences as discord, gossip, and backbiting. They feed on the burr of contention."[7]

I truly believe that the futurity of Church missionary work and retention depends completely upon the kindness and mercy of its members. People want to feel safe at church. They want a refuge from the storm. Joseph Smith once said, "The nearer we get to our Heavenly Father, the more we are disposed to look with compassion on perishing souls; we feel that we want to take them upon our shoulders, and cast their sins behind our backs."[8] Not judge them or condemn them.

If God looks on the heart, then we should too. If God is merciful to us, then we should strive to be merciful to others, regardless of how different they are from us. Our concern is not between God and others. Our concern is between God and ourselves, and God is going to look at how we've treated others as a measuring stick for how much we profess to love Him.

---

7 "Wolves in Sheep's Clothin [*sic*]," *Church News*, Sept. 6, 2003.
8 Joseph Smith, *History of the Church*, 5:24.

The Cultural Evolution

"By small and simple means are great things brought to pass."
—Alma (Alma 37:6)

Over the last few years, I've had the blessing and the curse of watching my blog go viral. During that time, I've had many experiences with people online and offline that leads me to believe that there's a cultural evolution taking place inside of Mormonism. This evolution is something that the prophets and apostles have been calling for in every passing general conference. We have been asked to improve culture—and everything that entails. This evolution will call out those who judge, those who hate, and those who refuse to see past their narrow, regurgitated, cliché points of view. This evolution will be an evolution of love and acceptance unlike anything the Church has ever seen.

Do you remember what was happening in Israel around the time that Christ came on to the scene? Israel had

19

started to live by their own set of oral laws and traditions, or what we might refer to today as "culture." The "culture" in Israel when Christ showed up was one of the most judgmental and hypocritical cultures the world had ever seen. It was a very isolated and unaccepting culture. But Christ showed up and cast a net over all types of people. The Greeks, the Romans, the Samaritans, and every other nation across the globe. His net covered even the worst of repentant sinners. The only people that were excluded or damned were the unrepentant elite, the "scribes and Pharisees, hypocrites" who "strain at a gnat, and swallow a camel" (Matthew 23:23–24). Christ brought with Him a cultural evolution of love, empathy, and compassion. He built a culture that was geared toward the lowly of heart and revolted against those who spent their lives pointing out the flaws in others. "For ye are like unto whited sepulchres, which indeed appear beautiful outward, but are within full of dead men's bones, and of all uncleanness" (Matthew 23:27). The bulk of Israel was living according to their culture and their superstition instead of their religion. This has been the bane of each and every covenant society, which caused Joseph Smith to say, "What many people call sin is not sin; I do many things to break down superstition, and I will break it down."[9] The doctrine of this church doesn't lose people. It's the culture and superstition that causes unnecessary strife.

---

9 Joseph Smith, in *History of the Church*, 4:445

I can imagine a time not too far off when a gay man, a straight man, a biker with full body tats, a woman who smokes, a man who reeks of liquor, a recently married couple who is having trouble with tithing, an excommunicated and recently re-baptized member, a man with a full beard and jeans, and a returned missionary who is addicted to porn, all sitting in the same congregation together, who make it through all three hours of church without someone dressing them down with their eyes or their words. It'll be a time when the stalwart multi-generational Mormon honors the saying on each of the signs that represent our Church: "Visitors Welcome." Not the sinless visitor, because Jesus said that the "whole need not a physician" (Matthew 5:31), but the visitor who comes with every last bit of weakness that they have. It'll be a time when the families in that congregation recognize how hard it is for people to set foot inside a church when they feel like they've strayed too far.

I'll never forget walking into a Michigan trailer park and knocking on the door of a woman who was on the records of the Church but hadn't been active in over twenty-five years. She had a husband now and a couple of kids. I still remember her sitting in a rocking chair, skin and bones, and tearful welcoming us in to sit with her and her husband. You could see that she had been ravaged by the years of drug use. When we asked her if she'd come to church with us, I'll never forget her response:

"I'll never set foot in church again. I've done too much. God doesn't want me in his house ever again."

I quickly opened up Alma 36, read a few passages from a prophet who had been to the depths of hell and back, and then assured her that she had not "done too much." We sat there as she began to cry uncontrollably. She rehearsed a life of sin unlike anything I had heard before . . . and said emphatically, "GOD DOES NOT WANT ME IN HIS HOUSE EVER AGAIN." It's not easy for people to come to church after a life of mental torment and anguish because of their past choices. They know that what they've been doing was wrong. They don't need someone else to remind them about it. When they do finally take that step forward, there's a good chance that this is the feeling of their hearts as they make their way through those chapel doors:

"I'm here because I need the help of the Savior . . . and I need your help. I'm here because I have no hope, no happiness, no family, and no friends. I'm here because I've hit rock bottom, and I'm here because the merciful hand of the Savior guided me this way through the power of the Holy Ghost. I'm here because the light that is within me has not been completely extinguished and I hope and pray that you will put some kindling on that fire and not extinguish it with your disdain for me."

I believe this evolution will produce an environment in which people always feel comfortable when they step inside a church building. It'll feel like home. They'll never have to feel like they've got to watch their back. They'll never have to worry about what sister so and so thinks about her outfit, or what brother such and such thinks about the fact that he returned home early from his mission. Those who have gone astray from the Church in their younger years will feel welcome when they come back to mend their wounds. They won't have to suffer the indignation of others who judge them for times long since passed and sins long since atoned for. The past history of a person will mean nothing to this new generation of saints. "Who are you now?!" is what we'll ask. Not "Who were you then?"

I wonder if people looked at the Sons of Mosiah and said, "Who do they think they are? How can they be missionaries? How can they represent Christ? How can they give advice in church when they were the vilest of sinners?" I wonder if those great missionaries were made to pay for their sins by their contemporaries, even though those sins had already been paid for. Because of these repentant boys' ability to overcome their past, they may have been the only Nephites alive who were willing and able to make an impact with those wretched Lamanites. It's the people who have lived through massive challenges in life—who have made major mistakes and have made themselves humble and vulnerable enough to empathize with others—who are able to reach "unreachable" people like those hostile Lamanites. And all of this revolves around love. Love passed from person to person to person. An extended hand, an arm around a shoulder, or a fervent prayer on behalf of an individual who has been through the ringer in life. Our culture needs a reboot. We need to pull for each other instead of being like the whiners in the parable Jesus gave about the workers in the vineyard. (See Matthew 20:1–16.)

One of the most influential senior missionaries I served with during my mission once told me that he loved the smell of alcohol and tobacco at church. He said, "It's the smell of change." There's someone sitting in that pew, trying to kick a habit, learning of Christ, and hoping for a friend to help take their mind off of that addiction . . . and yet some of us will move to the furthest pew and simultaneously say things that throw it right back in their face. This is bad! This is wrong! How can people do this or that! Slam! Whack! Bam! And the shame begins all over again for that struggling soul as they make their way back to their lonely apartment.

In this cultural evolution, I see a place where people have study groups to provide support for those who need friends to talk to about the things they hear on the internet and social media. I see a place where people support one another, ask questions, resolve concerns, and speak honestly about the things that give them trouble in life and in the Church. I see a time when home teaching is just referred to as "ministering" and more lessons revolve around love and not quotas. I see a time when "fellowshipping" will be replaced by "friendshipping" and when pure love is a stronger motivator than guilt.

I think this evolution will produce a people who don't make a checklist of things they can and cannot do on the Sabbath . . . and then hold others to their own standard and checklist. I think we'll see a time when programmatic meetings are cut by 50% and when the efficiency of those meetings are increased by 50%. We'll spend less time behind closed doors, meeting about all the stuff we should be doing, and more time ministering to the proverbial fatherless and the widows. We'll get back to true religion and root out any routine religion.

Members will increase their personal study of the scriptures. Missionaries will actually start memorizing scriptures so that there will be water in their wells. And callings won't be looked at as promotions where congratulations are in order. Any form of pageantry will die with this evolution during the uprising of the greatest generation of saints this world has ever seen.

I hope this evolution happens fast . . . because this world is in need of love, and that love will need to go out from Zion.

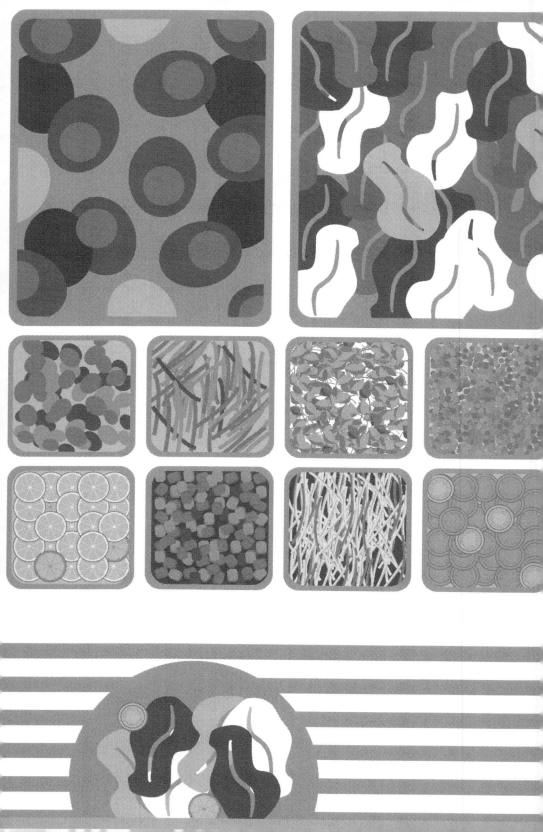

Customizing Christ

"Not every one that saith unto me, Lord, Lord,
shall enter into the kingdom of heaven; but he
that doeth the will of my Father which is in heaven."
—*Jesus Christ (Matthew 7:21)*

Please don't misunderstand what I suggested in the previous chapter. I'm not at all wishing for an "evolution" that brings about a degradation of the doctrine, the morals, or the values that have been the hallmark of this gospel for so many years. What I wish for, in a nutshell, is for people to be more loving to each other and more willing to overlook the weaknesses of the person sitting beside them. In no way am I saying that we should accept or condone the actions of those who persistently break the commandments of God. Loving people and not judging according to outward appearance is one thing. But playing the tolerance card to the point in which all lines are blurred is quite another. Too many people neglect what is in the scriptures and try to "customize Christ" into a Savior who requires nothing of those He has ransomed.

Too often we read a few scriptures that make us feel good and then omit everything else that we know about Jesus that might make us feel bad. Some have bowed down to modern trends and allowed themselves to be manipulated by the media and false teachers. Too many people look for a religion that is easy. In the world, we are offered instant salvation and taught about a Christ who accepts everyone just the way they are. There is no difference between our day and Isaiah's time when the people asked him to "Prophesy not unto us right things, speak unto us smooth things" (Isaiah 30:10). Instead of looking for a church that teaches truth, many are on a quest to find a church that can satisfy their innate desire to worship God and yet, at the same time, live the lifestyle that they want to live regardless of how ungodly it really is. Some consider it a great feat to find a church that allows them to live how they want to live and still feel like they are worshipping God.

I don't care whether you're Mormon, Catholic, Protestant, or any other type of Christian . . . one thing is for certain: the gospel of Jesus Christ is not a "buffet" that you can compile your perfect plate from. There is no salvation in building your own religion or customizing Christ to suit your needs and wants. The popular trend is to determine how you'd like to live your life and then to conform Christ to that lifestyle, appealing to Christ's infinite love and mercy. But you can't just go around rehearsing that "God is love" (1 John 4:8) and then be done with it. Likewise, John 3:16 is awesome . . . but it's just one verse! God wouldn't have given you all of those other verses if He didn't want you to read them and apply them.

At the base of this movement is the feeling that Christ was so loving and accepting of everyone that He would never stand for any kind of exclusion or discrimination. This could not be farther from the truth. Yes, it is true that Christ loves everyone, and yes, it is true that we should practice the doctrine of inclusion, but Christ was far from accepting behaviors that were not in accordance with the commandments. He didn't come to this earth and just "accept people" and let them act however they wanted to act. "Think not that I am come to send peace on earth: I came not to send peace, but a sword," He said, "For I am come to set a man at variance against his father, and the daughter against her mother, and the daughter in law against her mother in law. And a man's foes shall be they of his own household" (Matthew 10:34–36). In another place in the New Testament He even said, "I never knew you," as He spoke about people who were unwilling to repent and live the commandments (Matthew 7:23). How and why will "a man's foes be they of his own household"? Because Christ asks you to take a stand. He asks you which side of the line you're going to be on . . . and you prove which side you are on by "keeping the faith." Everyone and everything is not "ok" or "accepted" by Jesus Christ. All are loved by Him, but our behaviors have the power to leave us standing at a door which He will not open.

Does that sound all-inclusive?

If Christ were walking the earth today, preaching the same things He preached back in His day, people would be flying off the handle. He'd teach hard things. Draw a line in the sand. Tell people He loves them. Ask them to repent. Maybe even get mad and turn over some tables (see Matthew 21:12–13). Then they'd call Him a bigot. Self-righteous. Unaccepting of others and their ways of life. They would "go away" and start their own form of religion like so many of them did while He preached in Israel. The question you have to ask yourself is the same question He asked His apostles in John 6:67: "Will ye also go away?"

People get mad at the LDS Church, its leaders, and Mormons across the world for trying to defend some of the basic commandments. I'm amazed at the heat the Church gets for its stance on homosexuality or same-sex marriage. Christians inside and outside of the Church label Mormon doctrine as old and outdated and in the same breath say that Mormons don't believe in the Bible. Nothing in the Book of Mormon says anything about homosexuality. But guess where it is visibly forbidden? Paul tells the Romans, *in the Bible,* that "For this cause God gave them up unto vile affections: for even their women did change the natural use into that which is against nature: and likewise also the men, leaving the natural use of the woman, burned in their lust one toward another; men with men working that which is unseemly, and receiving in themselves that recompence of their error which was meet" (Romans 1:26–27). In the Old Testament, homosexuality was one of the primary reasons for the downfall of Sodom and Gomorrah. And again, Paul states that it is a man that should be with the woman "in the Lord" (1 Corinthians 11:11). That was biblical doctrine before it was ever something that needed to be addressed by the modern Church. Consider the woman taken in adultery in John 8. The Savior did not condemn her . . . but He also didn't condone what she did. He loved her and He forgave her, but He also meant what He said when He told her to "go and sin no more" (John 8:11). The forgiveness of Christ should not be misinterpreted for acceptance.

Mormons aren't trying to be exclusive or discriminatory toward anyone. If they are, then they are not living their religion. Elder Quentin L. Cook stated, "As a church, nobody should be more loving and compassionate. Let us be at the forefront in terms of expressing love, compassion and outreach. Let's not have families exclude or be disrespectful of those who choose a different lifestyle."[10]

We should be "loving and compassionate," but we should never allow ourselves to believe that Christ just accepts us how we are. That was never in the program. He's always asked us to change, to repent, to get better, and to overcome the things that we struggle with. When we quit trying to align our wills with God and start trying to get God to align His will with ours . . . that is when we start to lose our way.

Many people are taking the equality and fairness argument to the extreme, assuming that Jesus is accepting of everyone and everything. It's just not true according to the scriptures.

---

10 Quentin L. Cook, "In the News," *Ensign*, March 2013.

The Three Types of Mormons

"Gone are the days when a student asked an honest question and a teacher responded, 'Don't worry about it!' Gone are the days when a student raised a sincere concern and a teacher bore his or her testimony as a response intended to avoid the issue."
—*M. Russell Ballard*[11]

On June 16, 1844, Joseph Smith gave what is known as the "Sermon in the Grove." It was one of the last things we'd ever hear from the prophet and it got cut short on account of the rain. He was only eleven days away from his martyrdom at Carthage, and he knew that his time was drawing near. Before the rain ended the sermon, Joseph said something as applicable today as it was in 1844 Nauvoo: "I have reason to think the Church is being purged."[12]

---

11 M. Russell Ballard, "The Opportunities and Responsibilities of CES Teachers in the 21st Century," address to CES educators, February 26, 2016.
12 Joseph Smith, in *History of the Church*, 6:477.

When you combine that statement with a revelation given in Kirtland on July 23, 1837 (also known as Doctrine & Covenants 112), you get the feeling that it will not be an easy task to be a member of The Church of Jesus Christ of Latter-day Saints in the last days. The revelation states that "gross darkness" is covering the minds of the people and that "vengeance cometh speedily upon the inhabitants of the earth, a day of wrath, a day of burning, a day of desolation, of weeping, of mourning, and of lamentation" (D&C 112:23–24).

But what's most interesting is that so many of us assume that the secular world is going to take the brunt of these troubled times. That's not the case at all. In fact, the Lord says that "upon my house (Mormons) shall it begin, and from my house shall it go forth . . . first among those among you, saith the Lord, who have professed to know my name and have not known me, and have blasphemed against me in the midst of my house" (D&C 112:25–26).

So . . . I've observed three types of Mormons in the Church these days, but I believe that only the third type will be able to endure the trials of faith that are here now and are coming soon.

1. The Stalwart-but-Stubborn Mormon

These Mormons are full of faith and are used to the standard narrative. They cling to what they've learned in Primary and cringe at anything that might contradict the things they've learned for so long. Change is tough for this group of Mormons. They might quote the scripture that says "God is the same yesterday, today, and forever" (Mormon 9:9) and assume that the Church will also be the same yesterday, today, and forever. They still think that Joseph Smith sat at a table with a sheet between himself and Oliver Cowdery as he traced the engravings on the gold plates and translated for hours on end. They like how Abraham sought for further light and knowledge but have trouble applying that same principle to themselves. What they know . . . is what they know, and nothing else seems to matter.

This type of Mormon doesn't think much of Church scholars. They have their old library of books at home that consist of *Mormon Doctrine, Doctrines of Salvation,* and a host of other similar titles that were published between 1970 and 1985. They have the *Collected Works of Hugh Nibley* on their shelf but have a hard time getting through them. Critics of the Church would call these people "sheeple." They might sarcastically call them "TBMs" or "True Believing Mormons."

I love this group of Mormons. They are faithful and obedient. They always seem to be there to help and are generally service-oriented. Their only issue is how they might react to people that have questions about their faith. If the questions or statements they hear from others contradict or disrupt their long held understanding of something, they can sometimes get defensive and exhibit a condemning attitude toward the questioner. This behavior might make the questioner feel stupid . . . and can really turn off a struggling member that may have not had the same testimony building experiences that they have had. As Paul said, this stalwart but stubborn Mormon may have a "zeal of God, but not according to knowledge" (Romans 10:2), wherein they are immovable in their position on a portion of Church history or doctrine—but genuinely wrong all at the same time. Lots of zeal . . . but lacking correct knowledge causes the same situation Alma witnessed in the Church in his day. They "began to be scornful, one towards another, and they began to persecute those who did not believe according to their own will and pleasure" (Alma 4:8). These people have a major problem with just saying, "I don't know . . . but let's discuss," which leads to innocently but ignorantly misleading others who might be honestly seeking.

2. The Curious-but-Furious Mormon

This group of Mormons is small . . . but growing very fast because of the transparency of the internet and social media. They are good-hearted and sensitive people who have taken seriously the admonition of Joseph Smith to "go on to perfection, and search deeper and deeper into the mysteries of Godliness."[13]

But as they're searching, they're finding things that contradict the things they may have learned in Primary and Sunday School. Some of those things, as Elder Ballard has recently mentioned, are "less known or controversial . . . [such as] plural marriage, seer stones, different accounts of the First Vision, the process of translation of the Book of

---

13 Joseph Smith in *History of the Church*, 6:363.

Mormon or the Book of Abraham, gender issues, race and the priesthood, and a Heavenly Mother."[14]

Where the stalwart but stubborn Mormon might shun or ignore these topics and go about his or her business, the curious but furious Mormon might jump to wrong conclusions on incomplete information from less-than-reputable sources and make rash decisions regarding their faith. Once a person has made a rash decision, human nature and inherent pride make it very difficult to reverse that decision for fear of seeming "wishy-washy." Most of the time, when someone makes a rash decision, they end up getting behind their decision 100%, regardless of whether they know if it was right or wrong.

This type of Mormon is the one that approaches the other type of Mormon (the Stalwart-but-Stubborn Mormon) and asks them why the Sunday School manual has a picture of Joseph and Oliver sitting at the table with a sheet in front of them when in reality, Joseph used a seer stone in a hat to translate while the plates remained covered. If the stalwart but close-minded Mormon reacts defensively or arrogantly . . . a battle of truth vs. tradition ensues, and no one is the winner. In many cases, this type of Mormon is right about various aspects of Church history but doesn't stick around long enough to see the issue rectified in the upcoming manual. The curious Mormon now becomes a furious Mormon and believes they've been lied to maliciously for all

14 M. Russell Ballard, "The Opportunities and Responsibilities of CES Teachers in the 21st Century," address to CES educators, February 26, 2016.

these years . . . while the stalwart but close-minded Mormon has lost a brother or sister to help them run the ward council.

Both of these types of Mormons contribute to the attrition and declining numbers of reactivations and conversions.

3. The Stalwart-but-Curious Mormon

Ah, finally—a group of Mormons that are exciting to discuss. This group of Mormons consist of a marriage between the two previous groups of Mormons. Interestingly enough, blending the characteristics of the two above groups of Mormons makes the sort of Mormon who has the intellectual and spiritual ability to pull down the powers of heaven on a regular basis and work modern miracles. This is the sort of Mormon Joseph Smith was. This is the sort of Mormon who is firm in their faith but always open to discuss different points of view. They're looking for truth and willing to accept it even if it contradicts their current views. These are the Mormons who are truly learning and growing as they combine their faith and intellect to navigate through tough times.

These Mormons are more interested in helping people than they are at "being right." They are better at listening and understanding than they are at speaking and postulating. This type of Mormon has no illusions of the Church being perfect, the people or leaders being perfect, or the history being 100% accurate as recorded in a 1980s Sunday School manual. This Mormon is ready and willing to listen when Elder Ballard says you should learn about these controversial essays and topics and know them "like you know the back of your hand."[15] This Mormon knows that the narrative in the Church can change over time but that the doctrine can still remain pure and true and unlike any other theology this world has ever seen.

This is the true disciple of Christ. This is the peacemaker and knowledge seeker. This is the type of Mormon who will usher in the Second Coming of Christ. This is the type of Mormon I want to be.

---

15 M. Russell Ballard, "The Opportunities and Responsibilities of CES Teachers in the 21st Century," address to CES educators, February 26, 2016.

Doubters Welcome

"Except I shall see in his hands the print of the nails,
and put my finger into the print of the nails, and
thrust my hand into his side, I will not believe."
—Thomas, an ordained apostle (John 20:25)

Somewhere on the front of every Mormon church sits a plaque that reads, "Visitors Welcome." I sort of wish that there could be another saying on that plaque that would read, "Doubters Welcome."

Of course I want visitors or "non-members" to come to church, check it out, and be part of our great church family. But who I'm really missing right now are those who have already been part of that church family and have quietly slipped away because of doubt.

Many times, when people begin to doubt their faith, they start to believe that they are unwelcome at church. As if they'll be branded with some sort of scarlet letter on their chest.

Maybe church culture was like that in the past. But I am certain it's not like that in the present—and it won't be like that in the future. Everyone at church wants you back. Regardless of what you've done, or what you've said, or what you've believed or not believed, the Lord wants you to come back to the table and at a minimum . . . to be open to believing.

Sometimes, the sheer desire to believe is stronger than having a knowledge of things. Many people have acted contrary to the knowledge that they have received and fallen off the path, but rarely do you see someone who is striving to believe fall off the path. There is something powerful behind the concept of hope that drives actionable faith.

Elder Holland might be one of the most outspoken defenders of the Church, and yet he's recognized the need for doubters to remain welcome at church: "I think you'd be as aware as I am that that we have many people who are members of the church [sic] who do not have some burning conviction as to its origins, who have some other feeling about it that is not as committed to foundational statements and the premises of Mormonism. But we're not going to invite somebody out of the church [sic] over that any more than we would anything else about degrees of belief or steps of hope or steps of conviction. . . . We would say: 'This is the way I see it, and this is the faith I have; this is the foundation on which I'm going forward. If I can help you work toward that I'd be glad to, but I don't love you less; I don't distance you more; I don't say you're unacceptable to me as a person or even as a Latter-day Saint if you can't make that step or move to the beat of that drum.'"[16]

Most people don't realize that some of the greatest accomplishments in the Church have come from people who had doubts but were willing to continue to sit at the table with an open mind and work through their doubts. Each of Christ's apostles doubted that Christ would be resurrected. It was incomprehensible to them . . . even after having witnessed a man walk on water and raise the dead. All of the original apostles had doubts. Each of them, one by one, sat there witnessing the mighty miracles that came from this Nazarene. They had questions and problems with much of what Christ had taught, but their hearts were soft enough to allow them to keep coming back to the table. The problem exists when a person thinks that they are beyond faith. That they are too logical for miracles. That their intellect exceeds the need for faith. People who are honest enough to admit their doubts and then face them head on without becoming antagonistic, making hard-line rash decisions, or ruling out the need for faith are some of the greatest contributors to this kingdom.

I have always been the sort of person that likes to get to the bottom of things and research them for myself. That mentality is no different from those of Joseph Smith, Brigham Young, or many other great leaders of the Church. Blind faith has never been my thing. The leaders of every

---

16 "Interview Jeffrey Holland." The Mormons. April 30, 2007. Accessed September 20, 2017. http://www.pbs.org/mormons/interviews/holland.html.

age whom I respect the most never settled on someone else's word. They used a combination of logic and faith in order to arrive at their testimony and then never stopped building their testimony. They were never "finished" acquiring their testimony. We often attribute Brigham Young's testimony to coming from a single event wherein "a man without eloquence," Eleazar Miller, convinced him of the truth through his pure testimony—and pure testimony alone. But Brigham Young was a serious skeptic and doubter. For two years he hung around and observed, having obvious doubts . . . while keeping himself open to experiences that might solidify his faith. He said, "I wished time sufficient to prove all things for myself."[17] Yes, Eleazar's simple testimony may have sealed the deal for Brigham, but it was two years of careful observation and study that led him to a place in which his heart could be pricked by that simple testimony. Logic and faith finally intersected.

I'm a firm believer in what President J. Reuben Clark once said: "If we have the truth, it cannot be harmed by investigation. If we have not the truth, it ought to be harmed."[18] I've never felt like God has wanted anyone to display blind obedience. Sometimes we cite Adam saying, "I know not, save the Lord commanded me," as an example of blind obedience (Moses 5:6). But Adam's faith and obedience was far

---

17 Brigham Young, "A Discourse," Deseret News Weekly, 2 Oct. 1852, 96.

18 J. Reuben Clark, as recorded by D. Michael Quinn in *J. Reuben Clark: The Church Years,* (Provo: Brigham Young University Press, 1983), 24.

from blind. The guy was just in the presence of Heavenly Father and Jesus Christ and was booted out of the garden. He had that event fresh in his mind. He experienced first-hand the existence and reality of God. Many of us have not had the same firsthand experience Adam did. We're constantly looking for pieces of evidence to build our faith. It's that evidence combined with a humble faith that drives our testimony to endure through hard times.

Joseph Smith doubted all of the religions of his day. He questioned things maybe more so than any other man or woman that lived in this dispensation, and the result of those questions are what we have today as the Doctrine and Covenants. Alma's doubt caused him to literally fight against the Church for a time. But when he came back to church, he committed fully to the cause and said, "From that time (when he came back to the faith) even until now, I have labored without ceasing, that I might bring souls unto repentance; that I might bring them to taste of the exceeding joy of which I did taste" (Alma 36:24). Alma's doubt, hatred, confusion, and bitterness was replaced by love and devotion to the cause. Peter, James, and John fell asleep three times on the night the Savior needed them the most. But many of us fall asleep just once and never return.

Guess what the Savior did to the three apostles that fell asleep in Gethsemane: He turned them into his First Presidency and trusted them to take the gospel into the whole world. They fought through failure and doubt many times over and rededicated themselves to the cause again and again. Each time they got a little bit better and a little bit stronger . . . until at once, they became some of the most consistent and reliable disciples this world has ever seen. David O. McKay, B. H. Roberts, Gordon B. Hinckley—and the list could go on in these days with regular ol' people who have fought through serious doubt to become spiritual giants in the kingdom of God.

I can still remember when I fell asleep in the gospel for a short time in my younger years. I learned that having doubts doesn't require you to not have belief or faith. It's not an either/or. It's a journey from doubt to faith. An uphill climb—one that can be difficult at times. The world is constantly reminding you to do the easy thing by turning around and going right back down that hill of doubt. But if we go back down that hill, we'll never see the summit. Belief is what allows us to reach new heights, bless more lives, and attain a greater faith.

How would you like to be known for the next 2,000 years as "doubting Thomas"? Tradition has it that the guy preached the gospel for the rest of his life until he was speared to death in India. The only thanks he gets for his contribution to the Lord's kingdom is for everyone to refer to his name derogatorily.

Thomas gets a bad rap . . . but Thomas is actually one of the apostles whom I respect the most. I think we should give him a break. I think we should give all of the "Thomases" out there a break because things may not always be as they seem. People overlook the fact that this same Thomas was the one that said to his fellow apostles, "Let us also go, that we may die with him" in the face of being stoned to death for being with Christ (John 11:16).

But Thomas didn't become famous for that kind of bravery and loyalty. Instead, he became famous for his exchange with some of the other apostles when he said, "Except I shall see in his hands the print of the nails, and put my finger into the print of the nails, and thrust my hand into his side, I will not believe" (John 20:25).

All of the apostles were confused at the things the Savior taught. Their Jewish upbringing and understanding of the Messiah was not one that had Him hanging on a cross. They all believed He would liberate them from the Romans and from any of their oppressors. Not just die. So when he died . . . all of them had their faith obliterated. There was a twist in their faith that no one could explain at the current moment, but in time, it all was made clear.

Thomas was really no different than the rest of the apostles. Remember when the faithful women told the apostles that the tomb was empty and that the resurrection was a success? The scripture says that "Their words seemed to them as idle tales, and they believed them not" (Luke 24:11). This was all of the apostles, not just Thomas. Thomas just verbalized what everyone else was thinking. So it kind of stinks to have a 2,000-plus-year stigma on you for just saying what was on your mind.

The interesting thing to consider is that there was nothing malicious about any of the apostles' doubts. They truly wanted to believe . . . but were just having a hard time.

There is a difference between malicious disbelief and honest disbelief. Some people who disbelieve hate the things they used to believe in and hate that anyone else would believe in such things. That's why they become such ardent persecutors of those who continue to believe. But someone with an honest disbelief stays humble and open to whatever might happen next. The person who has doubts but a hopeful and believing heart says, "Help thou mine unbelief" (Mark 9:24). They continue to have hope, and they continue to exercise faith, which is what brought Thomas and the other apostles into that gathering in which Thomas was able to actually feel the wounds in His hands and in His feet.

Thomas—and the rest of the apostles for that matter—were in honest disbelief at the time. Thomas said he needed to "see to believe," but he still wanted to believe. He had no animosity in his heart. He loved the Savior. He loved the Church. He loved how he felt as he lived and breathed the gospel. But he had a little bit of doubt in his heart like so many of us do.

The bottom line is that the apostles didn't *know* if Christ was ever coming back. Even though He told them Himself that He would, they still had doubts. They *knew* a lot of other things. They knew they loved His teachings and they knew he performed many miracles . . . but there were still holes in their testimony that needed to be filled by future events on a later date. If the eleven remaining apostles held a testimony meeting on day two of Christ being in the tomb, none of them would have testified that they *knew* Christ was going to rise tomorrow. But it doesn't mean they gave up on Him.

They just didn't know.

And that's all right. If there are things you don't *know* . . . then it's sufficient to just have a belief. "*Belief* is a precious word," says Elder Holland, "an even more precious act, and [we] need never apologize for 'only believing' . . . . Christ Himself said, 'Be not afraid, only believe.'"[19]

If we're being honest with ourselves, we all have a little bit of Thomas in us. So take it easy on the Thomases out there. They might just be the next Paul . . . or Alma . . . or Amulek.

---

19 Jeffrey R. Holland, "Lord, I Believe," *Ensign*, May 2013.

The Kindness of Christ

"Behold, my bowels are filled with compassion towards you."
—Jesus Christ (3 Nephi 17:6)

The plan of salvation is known by many names and descriptions. It seems like everyone has a favorite. My favorite comes from 2 Nephi 9:6, where Jacob describes it as the MERCIFUL plan of the great creator. That word *mercy* is powerful. Sometimes I don't think we exercise that godly attribute of mercy as often as we should. The closest word that I can associate with MERCY is KINDNESS. It was the kindness of Christ that allowed Him to overlook our weaknesses, our mistakes, and our offense toward God. It was the KINDNESS of Christ that gave Him the ability to die for those who didn't agree with Him or didn't like Him or were annoyed by Him.

I sit in lots of church meetings with other leaders on a ward, stake, and regional level. I've come to realize that none of the things we talk about in those meetings really matter unless we are becoming more kind and merciful as a people. If we're not becoming kind people, merciful people, then we're not becoming like Christ . . . and nothing else really matters. It's all just going through the motions. We sometimes worry about calling, and rank and file and authority, and we have petty disputes about who's right, who's wrong, and who should win. It all distracts us from the one thing that we must become if we are ever going to be able to reside in the highest portion of the celestial kingdom: Christlike.

Perhaps one of my favorite teachings of Jesus Christ was given in just one simple phrase found in Matthew 23:24: why do you "strain at a gnat and swallow a camel"? the Savior asks the hypocritical Pharisees. In short, what good are all these "churchy" things if you never learn how to apply the KINDNESS of the Messiah to your brothers and sisters? If there is one thing we must learn from this great plan, it is how to be merciful and kind to others in their weakness or in our *perceptions* of their shortcomings. Sometimes we make a big deal over things that are trivial and unimportant. Sometimes we even do it at the expense of a friend. Sometimes we assume the worst about people when all the while we are begging and pleading for the kindness of Christ to be applied to us.

Not too long ago, I was asked to write a blog about the Sabbath day for LDS.org. I was blown away to find members, some who claimed to be former bishops or other leaders in the Church, hurl personal insults at me and about me because they didn't feel like I was qualified to write for LDS.org. They went on Facebook and other social media channels to express things they'd never say to someone face to face. They didn't even stop to consider whether or not what I had written contained things that were useful and true. They criticized what I had written not because they disagreed with what was written but because I was me. A nobody. A "blogger." Not a General Authority. Not a BYU scholar. Not important in their eyes. They had no idea that the whole project I was working on was done by invitation from the Church and under the direction of Elder Ballard. I experience things like this on a regular basis from critics of the Church. But it hurts so much worse when it comes from fellow members. Your friends. Your brothers and sisters in the gospel. I'm no Joseph Smith, but I remember feeling as Joseph felt when he said, "If my life is of no value to my friends, it is of no value to myself."[20]

As mentioned earlier, in a recent teachers' council meeting, I sat and watched a man censure a few humble sisters as they gave their suggestions on teaching by the Spirit. It was done in a very contentious and demeaning way. This was a leader in the ward, and from what I could tell, it was he who was doctrinally wrong while these sisters were right. When asked why he went about it that way in class, he said that it was his right and even his duty to criticize anyone who is speaking falsely. He said that unless he gets mad, no one listens. What happened to patience, long suffering, brotherly kindness, and the fruits of the Spirit? If this man thought

---

20 Joseph Smith, as quoted in Joseph Fielding Smith, *Essentials in Church History* (Salt Lake City: Deseret News Press), 374.

people weren't listening to him before, you can be certain they aren't listening to him now.

When I was playing baseball in college, I had a coach say something to me that I'll never forget. I think I'd been complaining about something in the dugout when this coach came up to me.

"Greg," he said, "There are two types of people in this life: there are fountains and there are drains. Which one are you?" He later told me that he took that saying from an old time hustler of a ball player named Rex Hudler. Rex was the epitome of optimism and people loved to be around him. Fountains are continually springing up, giving life and happiness to everyone that surrounds them. Drains, on the other hand, sit in the dark corners hiding from sight, always taking and never giving. They grow moldy and people might trip over them, unnoticed and incognito. No one ever takes a picture of a drain to remember for later. But fountains . . . fountains are framed and remembered for years to come.

This one concept is probably the most valuable things I ever got from the game of baseball. I think to myself on many occasions, "Am I a fountain or a drain?" Sometimes I catch myself being a drain. During those times, I've recognized that I'm unhappy. When I turn myself into a fountain, I recognize that I become happy. It's that simple.

Unfortunately, this world is full of drains. It takes less effort to be a drain and let the fountains do all of the giving. These drains spend every second of every day looking for an *i* to dot and a *t* to cross. They have no desire to dot their own *i*'s or cross their own *t*'s . . . only others'. They can't help but find fault, criticize others, and bring people down to their level in life. They destroy what takes years to build with a fit of rage or a slip of the tongue. It's almost as if they're just waiting for something to happen that they can "go off" on. They treat each bad situation in life as if it were personal, and the other person involved is trying to injure them. It's an "I'll show them attitude," constantly drawing that daily line in the sand, waiting, just waiting for someone to cross over or even come close to that line so that they can lash out. As President Gordon B. Hinckley once said, "There is nothing that dulls a personality so much as a negative outlook."[21]

We can't let this sort of thing creep into the Church and gain acceptance among members. For better or worse, people remember the things you say, and they may never be able to forget. Wounds to the body heal quickly, but wounds to the soul can linger forever. Our words often are the leading indicator on whether we'll be forever classified as a fountain or a drain. "Out of the same mouth," says James, "proceedeth blessing and cursing" (James 3:10). The voice that bears profound testimony, utters fervent prayer, and sings the hymns of Zion can be the same voice that berates and criticizes, embarrasses and demeans, inflicts pain and destroys their spirit and the spirits of others in the process.

Elder Joseph B Wirthlin melted my heart with his messages of kindness and mercy toward the end of his life. It seemed as if every talk he gave before he moved into the next life was engineered to bring more kindness and mercy

---

21 Gordon B. Hinckley, "Whosoever Will Save His Life," *Ensign*, August 1982.

into the hearts of the members of the Church. He humbly pondered some of the things he was witnessing late in his life. He said,

> I often wonder why some feel they must be critical of others. It gets in their blood, I suppose, and it becomes so natural they often don't even think about it. They seem to criticize everyone—the way Sister Jones leads the music, the way Brother Smith teaches a lesson or plants his garden. Even when we think we are doing no harm by our critical remarks, consequences often follow. I am reminded of a boy who handed a donation envelope to his bishop and told him it was for him. The bishop, using this as a teaching moment, explained to the boy that he should mark on the donation slip whether it was for tithing, fast offerings, or for something else. The boy insisted the money was for the bishop himself. When the bishop asked why, the boy replied, "Because my father says you're one of the poorest bishops we've ever had."
>
> The Church is not a place where perfect people gather to say perfect things, or have perfect thoughts, or have perfect feelings. The Church is a place where imperfect people gather to provide encouragement, support, and service to each other as we press on in our journey to return to our Heavenly Father. Each one of us will travel a different road during this life. Each progresses at a different rate. Temptations that trouble your brother may not challenge you at all. Strengths that you possess may seem impossible to another. Never look down on those who are less perfect than you. Don't be upset because someone can't sew as well as you, can't throw as well as you, can't row or hoe as well as you. Kindness is the essence of greatness and the fundamental characteristic of the noblest men and women I have known. Kindness is a passport that

opens doors and fashions friends. It softens hearts and molds relationships that can last lifetimes.[22]

One of the last things my grandma said to me before she died was, "How can I ever stand before my Heavenly Father unless I have been kind?" We can understand the plan of salvation and all the doctrinal details of the Creation, Fall, and Atonement . . . but if we aren't learning how to be merciful and kind to others, then none of that understanding matters. We fail—in all aspects—if we are not kind people. The very core of the plan of salvation is mercy and kindness, the kindness of Christ and the commission for us to learn how to become like Christ.

---

22 Joseph B. Wirthlin, "The Virtue of Kindness," *Ensign*, May 2005.

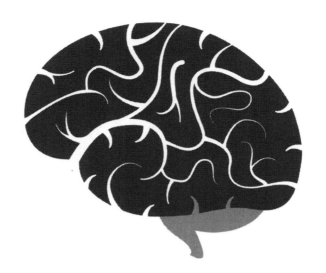

Embracing Intellectuals and Scholars

"The generations who succeed us in unfolding in a larger way some of the yet unlearned truths of the Gospel, will find that we have had some misconceptions and made some wrong deductions in our day and time. The book of knowledge is never a sealed book. It is never 'completed and forever closed;' rather it is an eternally open book, in which one may go on constantly discovering new truths and modifying our knowledge of old ones."
—B. H. Roberts[23]

S ome members of the Church believe that you can't be an intellectual and a Mormon at the same time. They might say that Mormons are "all heart and no brains." It's an insane accusation. There have been many notable intellectuals in the Church. Neal A. Maxwell, Jeffrey R. Holland, David A. Bednar, Hugh Nibley, or Joseph Smith, just to name a few. These are not dumb people. There are many

---

23 B. H. Roberts, *New Witnesses for God: Volume 3* (Salt Lake City: Deseret News, 1909), 503–4.

others in the Church that are committed researchers, academics, and scholars. In fact, many of the most solid members of the Church that I know of are serious intellectuals. These people aren't just going around "taking someone's word for it." They are continually battling, putting in the work and paying the price of discipleship. Mormons don't want to be fooled any more than anyone else does. So we thoughtfully, prayerfully, intellectually, and even sometimes cynically "study it out in our minds" first so that our hearts can be prepared for learning gospel truths.

Nephi said that in the last days, those who keep the faith will be few in numbers (see 1 Nephi 14:12), so it shouldn't be shocking to see a lot of people wavering. With wavering comes a lot of questions, and it's important to understand that no one is going to get mad at you or kick you out of the Church for questioning things.

The simple dictionary definition of an intellectual is someone who "has the ability to think in a logical way" and engages in "serious study and thought." I've tried to approach my faith intellectually according to this simple dictionary definition. I think most people who are serious about the Church have gone about it the same way. Why would I do it any other way? If "the glory of God is intelligence" (D&C 93:36), then I want to be more intelligent as it pertains to all of God's creations. But keep this in mind: no intelligent person ever became intelligent without asking a lot of questions and exercising an even greater amount of faith.

Hugh B. Brown had intellectual struggles. B. H. Roberts, Martin Harris, and Brigham Young had them, too. There are many notable leaders that had to work things out in their brain before the doctrine would take hold of their heart. No one is asking you or I to exercise blind faith or cast aside sound logic. In fact, the logic of Mormon doctrine is one of the things that appeals the most to me.

The key to intellectualism in the Church is found in the Book of Mormon. "To be learned is good," says Jacob, "if they hearken unto the counsels of God" (2 Nephi 9:29). But the problem is that so many people stop hearkening to the counsels of God as they become more learned. Sometimes, intellectual speed bumps become spiritual block walls when we stop keeping the commandments. When we start thinking that we're really smart or that we've got all the answers—that is when clarity of thought gives way to irrational thought. I think the worst mistakes are made when people jump to quick conclusions from incomplete facts and make rash decisions.

On the other side of the coin, there are honest truth seekers who are trying to "be learned" while simultaneously keeping the commandments of God. They're asking sincere questions and hoping for a sincere answer. We've got to welcome and embrace that mentality. Sometimes "faithful" members of the Church will look down on a person for asking tough questions. They might snidely tell them that "all that stuff isn't important to study" and to "just have faith." If it was like that in the past . . . then it's important to know that it's not like that anymore. Remember what

Elder Ballard said regarding some of the most controversial topics in the Church? You should "know the content in these essays like you know the back of your hand."[24] Not run from them or try to ignore them . . . but know them like the back of your hand. Generally, if people belittle a person for asking honest questions, it's because they don't have the answer themselves. Their own doctrinal insecurities get the best of them and pride sets in. Because they have deemed something unimportant for them to learn, they might suggest that it's also unimportant for the questioner to learn as well. Never should an honest question be met with scorn. It's never a good thing when other people try and dictate to you how and where you should receive your testimony. What may be unimportant to one person could be considerably important to another person.

One member scorning another for not having the same conviction as they do is counterproductive to every mission of the Church collectively and for individuals! When Alma experienced this in the Church of his day (as discussed earlier), this mentality became a "great stumbling-block to those who did not belong to the church; and thus the church began to fail in its progress" (Alma 4:8).

It's all right to have different perspectives on things, and it's not a bad thing to raise questions. It's the mode and manner in which a person questions things that makes all the difference, and it's the mode and manner in which a

---

24 M. Russell Ballard, "The Opportunities and Responsibilities of CES Teachers in the 21st Century," address to CES educators, February 26, 2016.

person responds to those questions that makes all the difference. Agitation is a far different thing from curiosity. People don't realize that Joseph Smith was the most inquisitive Mormon we've ever had in the Church. The guy was trying to learn all the time and from almost any source—many years after he had already translated the Book of Mormon and had many other revelations. He was always asking questions and looking for deeper meanings. He even chastened other members by saying that they needed to "drink deep" from gospel wells and that if the saints would apply themselves to more learning that God would reveal to them everything that had been revealed to him.[25]

You can be an intellectual and a Mormon. You can look at the doctrine logically, exercise faith, give serious thought and study to the Church, and still be a Mormon. In fact, intellectually spiritual members become the powerhouse teachers we need to help fortify the testimonies of those who are at the beginning of their journey with the Church.

---

25 See Joseph Smith in *History of the Church*, 3:380.

Change Comes Slowly

"Weary [the Lord] until he blesses you"
—Joseph Smith[26]

For some reason, when some people find out something about the Church that they did not previously know, they feel betrayed and believe the Church was trying to hide something from them. Then they make it their life's mission to expose every little mistake the Church or its leaders have made in the past to the present. But seriously, no one—ever—in this church has ever claimed that there haven't been mistakes along the way. What we do say is that the Church is a living church! Meaning that if a policy or interpretation is incorrect or just needs to be updated or changed, then the Lord can put us on the right track. That's what makes the Church true and unique. The Church is

---

26 Joseph Smith in Andrew F. Ehat and Lyndon W. Cook, *The Words of Joseph Smith: The Contemporary Accounts of the Nauvoo Discourses of the Prophet Joseph* (Provo: BYU Religious Studies Center, 1980), 15.

evolving and moving toward perfection in much the same way that we are. Line upon line, precept upon precept, here a little and there a little . . . but never all at once. Revelation takes place and change occurs inside the Church . . . slowly . . . for a reason.

The key to understanding this is found in Jacob. To me, this one little scripture is the most effective explanation at why change occurs slowly in the Church. When Jacob was recording the allegory of the olive tree, found in Jacob 5, he noted that the Lord is working in His vineyard, plucking, pruning, digging, grafting, and nourishing His Church. As the Church begins to grow, the allegory says, "ye shall clear away the branches which bring forth bitter fruit." But, says the allegory, the bitter will be replaced and cleared "according to the strength of the good and the size thereof; and ye shall not clear away the bad thereof all at once, lest the roots thereof should be too strong for the graft, and the graft thereof shall perish, and I lose the trees of my vineyard" (verse 65).

The Lord makes course corrections in His own time and for His own reasons but He is doing it "according to the strength of the good and the size thereof." Faulty interpretations, policies, and understandings are not uprooted all at once for purposes only known to God Himself. We see this happening all throughout the Old and New Testaments. I can think of so many ways this has been applied in the past and could be applied in the future, but the key is to wait upon the Lord.

It's no different than when ancient Peter gets rebuked over and over again by the Lord. Remember in Acts 10 when Peter is trying to determine who should and should not receive the gospel? Peter didn't think the gospel should go to the Gentiles, or any other nation for that matter, but because the Church was a "living church," the Lord had to tell him what's up! He had to tell him not once, not twice, but three times that he needed to change his view on who was to receive the gospel.

Peter contested, saying, "Ye know how that it is an unlawful thing for a man that is a Jew to keep company, or come unto one of another nation; but God hath shewed me that I should not call any man common or unclean" (Acts 10:38). Peter was under the impression that the gospel was only to be given to the "lost sheep of the house of Israel" (Matthew 15:24). And who could blame him for thinking this? It was Christ who said that He was not sent to anyone but the lost sheep of the house of Israel, meaning the Jews. Was Christ wrong? Was He being discriminatory or leading His own Church astray while He was on the earth? Of course not!

So, Peter was leading the Church according to the time he lived in and the knowledge that he had! He . . . was . . . learning! I hear people flipping out on Brigham Young because of something he said 200 years ago, but no one ever seems to question Peter or the Church that was established and running in biblical times 2,000 years ago. The Church, making course corrections in any age of the world through divine revelation, is one of the most obvious indications that the Church is actually true. The Lord is not going to just do it for us and fix every little issue all at once. He does it slowly, "according to the strength and size of the good."

The Lord corrects and rebukes Joseph Smith over and over again the Doctrine and Covenants. As time has elapsed, He's corrected Brigham Young and others many times over since the time the Church had been organized. He corrected Bruce R. McConkie, which caused him to say:

> Forget everything that I have said, or what President Brigham Young or President George Q. Cannon or whomsoever has said in days past that is contrary to the present revelation. We spoke with a limited understanding and without the light and knowledge that now has come into the world.[27]

In my opinion, this was one of the most important things Elder McConkie taught during his lengthy service as a scholar and a general authority. When it was all said and done, he humbly submitted that he was subject to the guiding hand of a living God and the revelations of the living prophet. This sort of course correction and associated humility from its leaders is a hallmark of the "true and living Church." We have no doctrine of infallibility in our Church. We believe that the Restoration is still taking place—even today—and that it will continue until the Savior comes to reign personally upon the earth. Having said all that, it's important to understand that the doctrine of Christ does not and will not change. There are certain doctrines that are

---

27 Bruce R. McConkie, "All Are Alike unto God," Brigham Young University devotional, August 18, 1978; speeches.byu.edu.

the same yesterday, today, and forever. These doctrines are central to the plan of salvation. Policy is completely different than doctrine. The doctrine of Christ taught within the scriptures and by the living prophets is what I have always rooted my faith in.

The Humble Few

"I beheld the Church of the Lamb
of God, and its numbers were few."
—*Nephi (1 Nephi 14:12)*

In the April 2017 general conference of the Church, it was announced that there were 240,131 convert baptisms in 2016.[28] This was the lowest number of convert baptisms that the Church has had since 1987, 30 years ago, when that number was 227,284 convert baptisms.[29] In 1987, we had 6,440,000 members on the records of the Church. Today, we're nearing 16,000,000. In 1987, we had 34,750 missionaries. Today, we have twice that. With double the amount of missionaries, you'd think we'd have many more convert baptisms than we did 30 years ago . . . but we don't. Those numbers are in decline, and there's no way around that fact. These stats seem to trouble a lot of people, especially those who were raised quoting Joseph Smith when he said, "This

28 Brook P. Hales, "Statistical Report, 2016," *Ensign*, May 2017.
29 F. Michael Watson in Conference Report, April 1988.

church will fill North and South America—it will fill the world."[30] We love to repeat that quote. It gives us validation and makes us feel good. We feel strength in numbers. But there are two things that we sometimes fail to consider. First, that miraculous prophecy given from a small log house with only a handful of people has actually been fulfilled. The Church has literally filled the world. And second, while the Church has filled the world, it doesn't mean that everyone is going to join the Church or that previous growth rates are guaranteed to continue. In fact, it might be the exact opposite. The scriptures tell us that in the last days, "our numbers will be few" (1 Nephi 14:12). It's going to become a real challenge for people to remain faithful to the Church and not acquiesce to the pressures of worldliness and the associated outlet and excuse to gravitate toward agnosticism and atheism. People don't want to be accountable to anyone anymore. They don't want to be accountable to their God, to their wife or husband, to their kids or grandparents, or to any type of ecclesiastical authority. People want to be their own God and make their own rules. And in all of this, none of us should be surprised. We knew it was coming.

In Doctrine and Covenants section 45, the Lord talks about the days we are living in right now. He talks about the times of the Gentiles being fulfilled and their rejection of the gospel and the missionaries. The pervasive description that he gives to men in these days is that of a failing heart. He knows exactly what they will say, "that Christ delayeth

30 Joseph Smith, as quoted in *Teachings of the Presidents of the Church: Wilford Woodruff* (2004), 26.

his coming" (verse 26). Just as the fullness of the gospel has hit its stride and there is worldwide accessibility to it, the people begin to "turn their hearts from [God] because of the precepts of men" (verse 29). Money, power, popularity, and the pleasures of the flesh become obsessions to people inside and outside of the Church. Technological arrogance and scientific elitism fill the air. Agnosticism and atheism become convenient scapegoats for those who want to "have a little fun," as they define it. "There shall be many which shall say: Eat, drink, and be merry, for tomorrow we die; and it shall be well with us" (2 Nephi 28:7). The carnal logic of these people will errantly conclude, "Meh . . . if I die and there is a God, then He is a merciful God and he will save me or else he's not merciful. But, eh . . . I don't even know if there's a God."

Every year of worldly scientific progress in this world is another step away from the "stories and fables" of a God in Heaven who created us, loves us, looks after us, and redeemed us. Millennials are leaving religion in hordes like a zombie infection in Time Square. One by one, they disassociate themselves with anyone or anything that might curtail their carnal desires. Your kids and mine, should they remain faithful to the Lord and His Church, will be among "the humble few" roaming the earth who will be able to shed light on the darkness. They will be the only ones who will have the power to bring clarity to all of the confusion. It will be up to them to carry a torch that has been dimmed by hundreds of years of Messianic absence. And truly . . . they will be few. They will need to reflect the strength conveyed in the words of Tennyson: "My strength is as the strength of ten / because my heart is pure."[31]

They will need to resemble the words of a nursery hymn that ran through President Thomas S. Monson's mind as he honored his faith as a youth in the Navy near the end of World War II.

> Dare to be a Mormon;
> Dare to stand alone.
> Dare to have a purpose firm;
> Dare to make it known.[32]

It was Nephi who saw the latter days and noted that "They have all gone astray save it be a few, who are the humble followers of Christ" (2 Nephi 28:14). And it will be the humble few who carry out and complete the evolution of love and faith as they anticipate and prepare for the Second Coming of Christ.

---

31 Alfred, Lord Tennyson, "Sir Galahad," *Poems: Vol. 2*, 1842.
32 Thomas S. Monson, "Dare to Stand Alone," *Ensign*, November 2011.

Millennial Mormons

"If you're living like there is no God . . . you'd better be right."
—Anonymous

Millennials are under attack right now. They get it from their schools, the media they consume, and the adversary himself. But dang it . . . we need those Millennials to be faithful and strong. They are the promised ushers of a new millennium!

Just to back things up a couple millennia ago, there was this guy in the Book of Mormon by the name of Korihor who really wanted to get rid of God. He went around making fun of everyone else for believing. He said that the people were foolish for having a hope in Christ or in God. He said that their belief was "the effect of a frenzied mind; and this derangement of [their] minds [came] because of the traditions of [their] fathers" (Alma 30:16).

He continued to spout off what we would call a twisted version of Darwinian evolution or the "survival of the fittest."

He said that there could be no atonement for sins and that all of us "prospered according to [our] genius, and that [we] conquered according to [our] strength" (Alma 30:17). He said that we could commit no crime because there was no God to whom we should be accountable to.

So . . . are we here by chance? Is there no purpose or meaning, rhyme or reason, to our existence here on earth? In 1802, a man named William Paley gave the analogy of stumbling upon a beautifully crafted watch and wondering where it came from.[33] Not only was the watch perfectly made, but the watch was working as well. Tick, tick, tick. Anyone in their right mind would never suppose that the watch assembled itself through blind chance. Even if the watch did somehow assemble itself, you've got to then ask yourself the question, "Who wound it up and set it into motion?" I'm sure watches were complex enough in 1802 for Paley to prove his point but if we fast forward to the year 2016, it's even more mind boggling. Let's replace Paley's watch with the brand new "smart watch" of your choice. If you stumbled upon one of these watches with all of its wondrous technology, would you ever in your right mind even consider that this watch assembled itself through blind chance? No logical person would consider it. They would assume that there had to be a designer of the watch that put all the parts together and then set it in motion.

---

33 See William Paley, *Natural Theology, or Evidences of the Existence and Attributes of the Deity* (1802), 1.

Paley's watch pales in comparison to a "smart" watch in regards to complexity . . . and yet a smart watch pales in comparison to the complexity of nature we see around us every day. The sheer act of reading this book or listening to this audio is a feat that cannot be replicated or explained by scientists. To have words mean something to you through an instrument called an eye and have information processed immediately in the brain and have that information create emotion throughout your body is a miracle. A miracle that cannot be replicated or explained away in a lab. There's not enough room in this book to expound upon the shortcomings of Darwin's theories on the origin of life or the vagaries of the modern evolutionary biologists. There's not enough room to lay out all of the historical evidence of the existence of Jesus Christ. And ultimately, there's little chance of convincing an atheist that there is serious evidence reconciling the biblical creation story to evolution.

Korihor acted as if he couldn't see the miraculousness of the world that surrounded him. He removed God from his mind and created, of himself, a god. He caused others to "lift up their heads in their wickedness, yea, leading away many women, and also men" to commit sexual sins, telling them that "when a man was dead, that was the end thereof" (Alma 30:18). He convinced them that it didn't matter what they did because they were just going to return to the dirt and become fertilizer, having no memory of even existing. He took away all hope of a future life and essentially told them to "live it up" while they were here.

It was all a garbage-filled lie.

So a prophet named Alma confronted Korihor and asked him in so many words what his stinking problem was. Korihor started to contend with Alma, baiting him for evidence of a God. Alma said a lot of things to Korihor, but none might be as poignant as these seven words.

"All things denote there is a God."

Alma continued, "yea, even the earth, and all things that are upon the face of it, yea, and its motion, yea, and also all the planets which move in their regular form do witness that there is a Supreme Creator" (Alma 30:44). An intelligent designer, if you will. The very cells of our bodies, invisible to the naked eye, have been compared to a well-orchestrated factory. There are approximately 37 trillion of these microscopic self-replicating factories keeping you alive. If you were to discard all that we know of the expanding and complex universe with all of its billions and trillions of galaxies and study only the human body, you can't help but believe in a Designer who knew what He was doing.

After a bad series of events for Korihor, he finally admitted that he "always knew there was a God" but that the things he believed and taught were "pleasing unto the carnal mind" (Alma 30:52–53). He did what so many people in our day do by shoving God into non-existence so that they can act however they want. Their initial desire to "be free" to act however they want backfires into a world of bondage unlike anything they ever could have imagined. The English politician and philanthropist William Wilberforce said it like this: "Christianity has been successfully attacked and marginalized . . . because those who professed belief were unable to defend the faith from attack even though its attackers' arguments were deeply flawed."[34] You see, people like Korihor like to ridicule people who believe that our world was created by an intelligent designer and that our lives have purpose and meaning. They consider believers to be irrational and illogical because they don't subscribe to the ever changing theories on the origin of life on our planet.

Some of the most vicious assaults on Christianity are taking place among young adults in our nation's universities. Many college professors are leading the charge to eliminate God, creationism, and intelligent design from the classroom, the campus, and the world. Millions of people go off to college looking for answers to life's greatest questions only to have their beliefs shaped by college professors who "profess" to know everything about anything. These professors passionately tell you that science can have nothing to do with religion and that to exercise faith in something you've never seen is irrational and illogical. Many unsuspecting students won't make it out of college with their faith intact. Ezra Taft Benson said that "one of the chief means of misleading our youth and destroying the family unit is our educational institutions."[35] It's a spiritual epidemic in which the result will be a society of people making their own rules and living their own laws. These professors and their protégés persistently attempt to prove that God is nonexistent, and

34 Modernized quote from *Real Christianity*, ed. Bob Beltz, (Ventura: Regal Books, 2006).
35 Ezra Taft Benson, in Conference Report, October 1870, 21–25.

that our world was created by sheer chance. Their *theories* are stated as fact, of course, because the guy pushing the theory is wearing a lab coat and calls himself a PhD.

These so called "facts" seemingly change with the release of every new textbook. Scientists and professors talk as if they know exactly how something happened and then proceed to persecute anyone for not believing the "evidence" they've produced. They drop it in a textbook, call it a fact, and then require you to believe it. In a couple years, another scientist comes along and "proves" that the previous scientist was wrong and submits his new theory as a fact subsequently requiring you to discard the previous "scientific fact" and believe the "new data." What I find most intriguing is that scientists have a myriad of conflicting explanations and theories about how life began. Many of them will even allow room in their realm of possibilities for the existence of an advanced and intelligent "alien" life that into their theories. They just won't allow themselves to call that "alien" life form "God." Many scientists have even suggested that these "aliens" were the ones to "implant" or begin life on this planet.

C'mon!

Funnily enough . . . scientists ridicule the concept of faith while simultaneously exercising their own form of faith on a daily basis. They're constantly placing their faith in their own unseen theories, seeking after evidence to vindicate their assumptions of the natural world. As Elder John Widtsoe pointed out, "Science requires a strong faith in 'things not seen.' "[36] Did you realize that the scientifically accepted building blocks of life have never actually been seen? We learn about the proton and electron and other subatomic properties, and yet no scientist has ever witnessed their existence. They say that there's enough evidence to prove the existence of these subatomic properties, and yet they remain invisible.

Interesting. Very interesting.

But faith is just the beginning. Scientists even have their own form of repentance. Every time one of their experiments fail, they "repent" or "turn" from the error of their way and go back to the drawing board attempting to do it better the next time while they exercise more faith in unseen properties and their "educated guesses." For some reason, faith in God or an intelligent designer is not feasible for them. They strive to prove through science that God doesn't exist but they've failed miserably. In fact, the more that is discovered about life and about our universe, the more it seems to prove that God does in fact exist.

My hope is that the Millennial Mormons recognize how important they are in the context of the preparation of the Second Coming, and that they are intellectually persistent enough to fight through the barrage of supposed scientific facts that purport to render their life completely meaningless.

---

36 John A. Widtsoe, *Joseph Smith as Scientist: A Contribution to Mormon Philosophy* (Salt Lake City: Young Men's Mutual Improvement Associations, 1909), 76.

Rash Decisions

"A fool hath no delight in understanding,
but that his heart may discover itself."
—*Proverbs 18:2*

The Church of Jesus Christ of Latter-day Saints is unique. Its core beliefs revolve around the idea that there are prophets in the land again and that the heavens have been opened once again. It differs from the Catholic and Protestant beliefs that the heavens are closed and that the canon is complete. While most Christians believe that the Bible is the infallible word of God, Mormons (who are also Christian) believe God has once again returned to the earth to set the record straight and give us ongoing "further light and knowledge." While each of us can receive personal revelation for ourselves, our families, and our stewardships. The prophetic "keys" to receiving revelation for the Church is the responsibility of the living apostles.

Some of those apostles are pretty old. Ok, ok . . . most of them are pretty old. So here are the big questions:

Are those apostles we call "the Brethren" too old, irrelevant, and out of touch with reality? Are they fit to be leading a church, and should you listen to them?

As of late, there have been a good number of people who have raised their voice online and in the media to challenge the Apostles both inside and outside of the Church. They want them to catch up with the times and "adjust this doctrine" or "change that policy."

The Quorum of the Twelve are not a bunch of dumb old guys sitting in a windowless office somewhere in a Salt Lake basement. If anything, their ages have helped them see more of the world and become more wise and prudent in their decision making. But where you might see only twelve or fifteen "aged" men shaping policy, receiving revelation, and providing instruction, I see a supporting council of some of the best and brightest men and women this world has to offer. The Quorums of Seventy that span the globe are no slouches, either. The mission presidents, temple presidents, and stake presidencies around the world are the cream of the crop. This is not an uninformed group of people, and the members of the Quorum of the Twelve are carefully considering it all.

These are cool, hip, modern, successful, and wise people who are thinking things through and not making rash decisions. Each of them are seeking the will of the Lord in the decisions that they make and trusting that the Lord is at the helm. I just wonder if it has ever occurred to people who challenge the Apostles that maybe, just maybe, the Apostles know something that they don't.

Do you remember when Captain Moroni absolutely goes off on Pahoran in Alma 60? Moroni and Helaman are fighting for their lives on the battle front against the Lamanites. Pahoran is the chief judge of the land, located in Zarahemla. Moroni and Helaman badly need supplies and men to give them relief on the front. Moroni writes to Pahoran for relief, but Pahoran sends them nothing.

So Moroni goes off:

"We desire to know the cause of this exceedingly great neglect; yea, we desire to know the cause of your thoughtless state . . . [while you] sit upon your thrones in a state of thoughtless stupor" (Alma 60:5–7). He goes on to call them "traitors to [their own] country" (verse 18). After even stronger language, he ends by declaring, "I seek not for power, but to pull it down" (verse 36).

Sound familiar? See any relation to our day? Moroni was a faithful "member," if you will, on the outside looking in. He wanted change, and he wanted it now, and he was willing to freak out on Pahoran to get it without knowing all of the facts first.

I'm not trying to take anything away from Moroni here because I love Moroni . . . but Moroni was completely wrong in this instance. His writing was powerful, his words elegant, and there's no doubting his commitment to God and country. "If all men had been, and were, and ever would be, like unto Moroni," the record says, "the very powers of hell would have been shaken forever" (Alma 48:17). Moroni was an obvious stud. There's no question about that.

But Moroni was about to erroneously revolt and march against his own governor, his own land, and his own people. Moroni didn't have the whole picture. He assumed something incorrectly, and were it not for the wisdom of Pahoran, Moroni could have caused an unnecessary disaster for himself, his men, Helaman, and his entire nation. Not an ounce of guile was in Pahoran's voice as he replied to Moroni's misguided rebuke, saying, "In your epistle you have censured me, but it mattereth not; I am not angry, but do rejoice in the greatness of your heart. I, Pahoran, do not seek for power, save only to retain my judgment-seat that I may preserve the rights and the liberty of my people" (Alma 61:9).

Fortunately, Pahoran's letter reached Moroni before he made any unfounded life-changing moves on Pahoran and the capital. But what if Pahoran's letter never reached Moroni? Moroni might not be the hero he is today, and the Nephite history might have ended in Alma 63 with civil war. All from an unfounded assumption.

I just wonder how many men and women, "Captain Moronis," are out there in the Church right now with unlimited potential to lead and inspire but have jumped to wrong conclusions about current doctrines and policies. They want change, and they want it now—and if it doesn't happen now, then they assume that the Apostles are just old fashioned, slow to act, and sitting around in a "thoughtless stupor" all day. That is not the case. And just like Captain Moroni, if we could see the entire picture of what Pahoran was dealing with, we might structure our language and our letters a little differently.

The beauty of the Restoration is that it's still taking place . . . and I'll bet if you're patient, you'll receive that metaphorical "letter from Pahoran" in the near future. It will shed light into persistent questions and bring comfort to your soul in knowing that the Lord has been, and still is, guiding His Apostles in these last days.

Giving Volunteers
a Break

*"Any fool can criticize, condemn, and complain—
and most fools do. But it takes character and
self-control to be understanding and forgiving."*
—*Dale Carnegie*[37]

So . . . what happens when a person gets called to a leadership position and it's your opinion that this person is not fit to lead? Maybe you've know them personally, and based on what you've witnessed in the past, you can't believe that the Lord would actually want them to preside over you and others. You've never seen them commit any type of grievous sin or break any sort of law, but you just can't believe that this person would be called to lead!

When this happens, it can and has become a real issue for many people. It might cause you to doubt the validity

---

37 Dale Carnegie, *How to Win Friends and Influence People* (New York: Simon &Schuster, 1936), 36.

of a calling or the method through which the calling was issued. It might make you wonder why God would choose "this person" to preside over other people when you've witnessed what you would consider less than stellar behavior from that newly called leader. You might think to yourself, "If they knew what I knew, that person would have never been called to that position."

So what do you do?

Some people go berserk. They stew and fret and obsess over this one individual and their newfound authority. It might cause them to stop coming to church or seek an exception to the ward boundaries.

Don't do that. . . .

Regardless of how you feel about your recently called leader, if he or she has asked you to do something that will please God, then just do it. Why not, right? You can't go wrong when you're doing good things regardless of who is asking you to do them. If you believe the request to be unrighteous, then ask to speak with the leader privately in order to preserve his or her dignity in front of others. Never start badmouthing that leader to other members behind their back. If you yourself would ever like to be a good leader, you should know that good leaders are never gossipers. They don't go behind others backs or try to "gather others to take their side" to help justify their feelings toward another person.

The Savior gave an outline on how to handle these disagreeable situations. He said, "if thy brother shall trespass against thee, go and tell him his fault between thee and him alone: if he shall hear thee, thou hast gained thy brother. But if he will not hear thee, then take with thee one or two more, that in the mouth of two or three witnesses every word may be established" (Matthew 18:15–16).

How you handle yourself in these situations will determine the type of leader you will become. In fact, it is the defining character attribute of the greatest leaders to turn bad situations into good ones. It could be the single hardest thing you learn how to do in your life, but if you can "change frowning foes to smiling friends,"[38] then you will be classed among the greatest leaders this earth has ever seen, regardless of your current title or position.

Don't let your perceptions turn into grudges. Grudges into fights. Fights into wars. That person that bugs you so much is your brother or sister and a flawed human just like you.

Their calling to lead doesn't diminish your ability to lead. In fact, some of the best leaders show their true leadership abilities at the times when they're not holding prestigious titles. Good leaders are always the best followers. You might be able to help, influence, and lift the person who was just called to that position.

Many of those who are called to leadership positions in the Church are not necessarily prepared to serve in the capacity that they've been called to. Some have never served in a single leadership position in their life. They may not know what to do, and they might be completely overwhelmed.

---

38 "Savior, Redeemer of My Soul," *Hymns*, no. 112.

They're probably confused and scared and possibly as dumb-founded are you are that they were called to that position.

So help them, forgive them, support them, sustain them, and get to know them. The more you get to know them and understand them, the more you might come to love them.

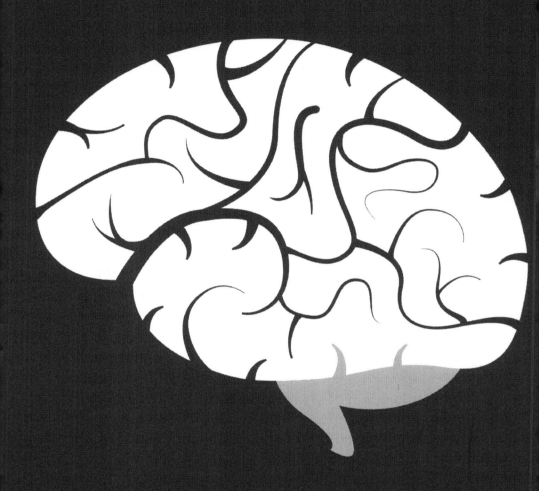

Logical Evidence
Is Mounting

"There will be a convergence of discoveries to make plain and plausible what the modern prophets have been saying all along."
—*Neal A. Maxwell*[39]

C ritics say that Mormonism was orchestrated by a man. Mormons say it was orchestrated by God. My goal was to find out. I needed to find out if this orchestration was beyond the reach and scope of a man. So I started looking at the various "coincidences," important dates, and what I would consider impossible occurrences that took place as part of the coming forth of the Book of Mormon and subsequent restoration events.

The day before Joseph Smith was born was the twenty-second of December, which is the "Winter Solstice," the shortest day of the year. That day has the least amount of

---

39 Neal A. Maxwell, "Discipleship and Scholarship," *BYU Studies* 32, no. 3 (Summer 1992), 5.

light, making it the darkest day of the year. The dawning of the next day, December 23rd, marks the beginning of brighter days! That day is a symbol of new beginnings and greater light.

Now imagine that! Joseph Smith was born on the one corresponding day of the calendar year that brought brighter days on to the earth in his region of the world. But let's dig even deeper. The woman who brought Joseph Smith into the world was named Lucy. The name Lucy comes from the Latin meaning of "light" or "light bringer" or "light bearer." So this "light bringer" lady happened to bring a boy into this world whom she named Joseph. Did she realize that when she named her fifth child Joseph, that the Hebrew meaning of his name meant "God will give increase" or "God will add to"? The boy's last name would be a Smith. What is a "smith"? A smith is someone who forges and builds something new out of old and raw materials. Let's take it even further. The boy Joseph had an older brother who stood by his side even until death. His name was Hyrum. The name Hyrum in the Hebrew means, "my brother is exalted" or "brother of the exalted one."

This thing we call the Restoration is much more elaborate than most people suppose. It was orchestrated by someone. That many coincidences don't just line up this way. It was either orchestrated by God or man. If it was orchestrated by man, then it was the most complex and comprehensive hoax to ever take place. But you've got to ask yourself, is there any way that any of this could have been orchestrated by man, especially when so many of these "coincidences" were set in motion well before any of the key players were born? Did Lucy's parents name her Lucy and then ensure that her third child was then named "Hyrum," so that he could stand by her fifth son who was named Joseph, whom she would somehow cause to be born on the Winter Solstice, the one day of the year that most accurately codified what a prophet of a new dispensation would do (bring new light)? Could they have known? Is it humanly possible? I can't see how it would be.

But that's just the beginning of the miracle of it all.

Now it was the angel Moroni's turn to provide some evidence for us to stumble upon in our studies. Joseph Smith reported that Moroni initially visited Joseph and subsequently gave him his first glimpse of the gold plates on September 21, 1823. That date coincided with the Feast of the Tabernacles. The Feast of the Tabernacles was instituted by God as a way for the Israelites to commemorate and remember the deliverance of God in times past. Out of all the times of the year, could there have been a better day for God to reveal a book that would mark the beginning of God's final deliverance and gathering in the last days? Could Joseph or Lucy or Lucy's parents or anyone else even have a chance to get that right? Were they academically capable of that kind of historical orchestration and planning?

If you just look at the significance of the names, the dates, and the setting of this latter-day restoration, you can logically conclude that there is more than just coincidence at work here. You'll also be able to conclude that there is no way this orchestration came about by any human. No human is capable of setting up that many coincidences BEFORE they were even born. But this is just the tip of the coincidental iceberg. We could talk about the importance of the Malachi statement, Church organization dates, and the miraculous appearance of Elijah in the Kirtland Temple on the exact date that Jews around the world were setting a table for the Passover meal and leaving an empty chair at the table for Elijah to return. We could go on and on and on.

One of the greatest evidences in my mind of Joseph Smith being a prophet is the fact that there are so many of these cosmic coincidences associated with the coming forth of the Book of Mormon and surrounding events of the Restoration. It's one thing to make a prophecy and then go out and fulfill that prophecy, but it's quite another thing to have meaningful evidence lined up to prove your case before you are even born.

In the past, it was only the prophets of the Bible who were born into these types, symbols, and foreshadowing. These were things that would give us evidence of a Creator and point our minds to Christ. These were things that could only be prepared for them from before the foundation of the world and not by any human in this temporal world. "God has a work for you to do," said the angel to Joseph Smith, "and your name will be had for good and evil among all nations, kindreds, and tongues, or that it should be both good and evil spoken of among all people." (See Joseph Smith—History 1:33.) Who says that . . . and actually has it happen?

God asks us to study things out in our minds (see D&C 9:8), to take a step forward, and then ask Him if it's right before we ever fully accept or commit to something. Never have I come across any of the Lord's teachings in which He doesn't want us to use our brains. I feel like our intellect is much more important than we've given it credit for in the past. God said He would tell us in our *minds* and in our hearts (D&C 8:2–3). But we spend a lot of time talking about how to "follow our hearts" or "listen to our hearts." God speaks to us first through our minds, and then our minds subsequently convey peace to our hearts. It is the feeling of light cleaving unto light (see D&C 88:40) that illuminates our bodies and gives us peace in our hearts. Joseph Smith once said, "When you feel pure intelligence flowing into you, it may give you sudden strokes of ideas . . . [and] those things . . . were presented unto your minds by the Spirit of God."[40] From what Joseph Smith is describing, our minds and our associated God-given intellects are at the core of our eternal progression. It is not our intellects that deceive us. It is our agency, rebellion, and rejection of the feelings that have been transmitted to our heart through the instrumentality of our brain and the spirit that quickens it (see D&C 45:26). The intellect just conveys. It's the heart that accepts or rejects.

Humans are prone to forgetfulness. I believe that is why so many prophets have emphasized the importance of the word "remember" over the years. It's easy to forget the

---

40 Joseph Smith, in *History of the Church,* 3:381.

things "we absolutely knew to be true" just a couple years ago. So we've got to continually search and seek and remember the things that brought peace to our hearts through the instrumentality of our minds so that we can stay sturdy and strong in these last days. I find that if you look hard enough, you'll be able to see that the Creation and orchestration of the Restoration of the gospel has plenty of logical evidence built in to reinforce our faith. Long before Joseph Smith even set foot on earth, orchestration was taking place. We just have to see it, recognize it, and attribute it to the correct source.

From Which All Others Are Derived

"Every dispensation of the past is like a great river.
The present dispensation is like a great ocean. All of the
rivers of the past flow into the ocean of the present."
—*Bruce R. McConkie*[41]

Some people wouldn't consider Mormonism a world religion . . . but it is. Mormonism is Christianity at its core. It's a restoration of the Church that Christ established when He was on the earth. What really makes the Church unique is the fact that it's the only religion on earth that I know of that tries to embrace all of the other world religions for the truth that is contained within them.

When I was in college I took a world religion class and loved every minute of it. The professor was an evangelical PhD of religion. I think it was the best grade I ever received

41 Bruce R. McConkie, "The Gospel Restored," *New Era*, December 1976.

in a college class. The class provided a deep analysis of the roots and teachings of the great religions in the world.

Every single class, my friend and I would look at each other in amazement as the doctrines of the Mormon Church were taught over and over again. Primal religions, Hinduism, Buddhism, Sikhism, Jainism, Confucianism, Taoism, Judaism, Islam, and Christianity in all its 40,000 different denominational variations. Each of them containing pieces of truth.

It makes all kinds of sense if you think about it. In the beginning, God gave the gospel to Adam and Eve. They taught their children the fullness of the gospel and there was only one "church" on the earth at that time. Who can dispute that?

Over the years, some of the sons and daughters of Adam and Eve started to fall away from the teachings of the Church, resulting in various tribes and people being scattered across the earth. These people started civilizations of their own but still retained their innate desire to worship a deity, so . . . they started their own religions. Many of these individuals, being good people, took the traditions that were passed down by their fathers and built a belief system based on their recollections of the traditions. Those traditions became appealing to the people in their geographic region.

I remember when this religion professor first started teaching us about the traditions of the Australian Aborigine, one of the oldest known primal religions. Apparently their roots go back to a creation event they call "The Dreaming." It was when their God-like/angelic *ancestors* came to earth and gave rise to the lay of the land, the animals, and customs/teachings *before the humans inhabited* it. It was also interesting to hear that they had various rituals that were required in order for them to understand "The Dreaming."

Then I opened up the Pearl of Great Price to read the Mormon understanding of the Creation, which says, "And there stood one among them that was like unto God, and he said unto those who were with him: We will go down, for there is space there, and we will take of these materials, and we will make an earth *whereon these may dwell*" (Abraham 3:24; emphasis added).

Whoa! That's cool. How could it be that a primal religion that goes back almost to the beginning of recorded history and Mormonism could have such similar beliefs about creation? Premortal Gods/angels organizing already existing materials into an earth for us to dwell on? Mormons embrace that kind of stuff, not condemn it!

How about Hindu's understanding of a premortal existence? Their concept of karma is the results of premortal actions. Mormons have a similar concept of being "called and prepared" before the foundations of this earth, just as the Jeremiah was ordained before he came to earth. (See Jeremiah 1:5.)

Those are just a couple examples. I could go religion by religion for pages upon pages and pull out the pieces of truth that match up with LDS doctrine. Study the religions of the world and visit some of their temples and synagogues and then attend the LDS temple a few times and your head will be spinning from the undeniable parallels you'll see with the religions of the world. I don't know of another religion in the world that is so interested in other belief systems and so ready to accept their teachings as inspired from God.

Truly, Mormonism is universal in its scope and adoption of truth.

Mormonism seeks to do just one thing: search the world for truth and then embrace it—whether it is found in the Texas mega-church or in the Tibetan desert. Mormons don't slam the door in another person's face or create literature to slam other religions, because they genuinely feel a common bond with so many of the truths found within those other religions.

A few years ago, Gordon B. Hinckley was asked to speak at a convention of the Religion Newswriters of America. After his talk he was asked, "What are you going to do when 15,000 or 20,000 Baptists visit you in Salt Lake City next summer and try to proselytize you?"

He replied, "We are going to welcome them. We are going to do everything we can to make them feel at home. These are our brethren and sisters. They accuse us of not being Christian. I hope that our people will try to show them, by the very manner in which they act, that we are truly disciples of the Lord."[42]

---

42 Gordon B. Hinckley, "The BYU Experience," Brigham Young University devotional, November 4, 1997; speeches.byu.edu.

Then he said this simple phrase that really captures the essence of Mormonism: "You bring with you all the good that you have, and then let us see if we can add to it."[43]

---

43 Gordon B. Hinckley, as quoted in "Messages of Inspiration from President Hinckley," *Church News,* Nov. 7, 1998, 2.

Temple Workers Galore

"To accomplish this work there will have to be not only one temple but thousands of them, and thousands and tens of thousands of men and women will go into those temples and officiate for people who have lived as far back as the Lord shall reveal."
—*Brigham Young*[44]

I was sitting in the room as a temple officiator, about to begin an endowment session, when I was overcome with emotion as I looked at the attendees of that session. I saw people of all shapes and sizes, colors and ethnicities. There were young people who looked strong and vibrant. There were old people who could barely sit or stand. There was a man in an electric wheelchair, a smile beaming across his face. I couldn't help but ask myself, "What are these people doing here in this temple? Why are they here? What motivates them to do this?" Then I turned inwardly and asked myself, "Why am I here spending so much time in this temple?"

---

44 Brigham Young, in *Journal of Discourses*, 3:372.

I can't answer those questions for anyone else but myself . . . but I personally love going to the temple for two reasons. One of those reasons is based on how I *feel* when I'm there, and the second reason deals with the things I *learn* while I'm there.

I wish the world knew that the temple is not weird. To atheists, every religious ceremony is weird, so it would be really hard for me to make a case to them about it. They go to biology class and learn about how the universe was created by chance or by aliens or whatever. I go to the temple to learn about how the universe was created by an intelligent designer who carries the name and title of God. "Weird" is just defined by a person's perspective, and some people think a Mormon temple is weird. That's all right. But for Bible believers . . . I can make a case for the temple being anything but weird.

There's this little obscure trio of verses found in the book of Revelation that most people pass over. In these verses, John is seeing in vision the last days, and in this vision one of the elders comes up to him and essentially asks him, "Who are these people dressed in white robes, and where did they come from?"

John defers back to the elder in the vision for the answer: "These are the people who came out of great tribulation and have washed their robes, and made them white in the blood of the Lamb." Meaning, these are some people that have dedicated their lives to God and have had the Atonement of Christ become active in their lives. The elder continues telling John about these people. These people are in God's house and they "serve him day and night in his temple" (Revelation 7:13–15).

Personally, I don't know of any other church that fulfills this New Testament prophecy. I watch people coming in and going out of the temple "day and night" as they serve the Lord in His house on earth. If you believe in the New Testament, you've got to scratch your head and wonder if those Mormons are on to something.

Many of those workers in these temples are women. These women officiate in the ordinances of the priesthood. I loved this when I first realized it. It opened up to me an entirely different view of the priesthood. Just last night, my wife and I went to the temple and she pointed out even a few more areas in which women participate fully. Women not only participate in every major performance and ordinance but they are also required to be present and active in order for the ordinances to continue. Not optional but essential. The ceremony, the covenants, the ordinances . . . all of it would crumble without women.

We learn that Eve was amazing and wise and that through her instrumentality and thoughtful consideration, all of us now exist. All of us now have the opportunity to learn and progress toward our potential. Women were the Lord's crowning creation, and from the very beginning we stood in awe, giving respect to them above all other creations.

As we come to more fully understand the roles of both men and women in the priesthood, our minds are then taken to what should be the center of our worship. The temple—every part of it—is the greatest earthly symbol we have of Jesus Christ. Every step of the way in the temple, we're met with things that point our minds back to Christ. The words, the ordinances, the architecture, everything, if you look for it, will bring your mind to an appreciation of Jesus Christ. In the last verse of that same chapter in the book of Revelation we discussed above, John records that the Lamb (Christ) would be in the midst of them and that He would feed them and "lead them unto living fountains of waters: and God shall wipe away all tears from their eye" (Revelation 7:17).

My wife observed a man in the temple bound to a wheelchair who seemed to be having a hard time. She told me of how this man maintained a smile unlike anyone she had ever seen. He could easily justify staying home and no one would second guess him. It melted her to tears as she thought of what this man has had to go through and what he is still going through . . . and yet here he was, dedicated, committed, and beaming in the temple! She could see the enabling power of the Atonement radiating from this man in his permanent chair.

God is in His house, wiping tears from their eyes.

The driving force behind the temple work is a bunch of old people. Without their willingness to serve instead of retire into idleness, much of the work on behalf of our dead would never move forward.

Recently I took a few missionaries to a session with me. Among us was a man that must have been in his late 80s or early 90s. He was moving very slowly, trying his best to get through the session. Eventually, we made it into the celestial room and when I walked in, I was shocked by what I saw next. The man's pants had fallen to the ground and he was so old that he couldn't even pick them up. It must have been embarrassing for this man to have this happen to him. One of the elders helped him out and everyone tried to remain reverent in that holy room, but inside I had so many emotions going through me.

For one . . . it was funny. I couldn't help but think it was funny. I don't think anyone could resist an internal laughter. The missionaries and I had a good laugh about it on the way home. But that laughter (not loud laughter of course) was replaced by a profound reverence and respect for these latter-day warriors. This guy was an extreme example, but I watch people like him come in and out of the temple every time I'm there. Instead of rotting away on their couches, they practically crawl their way to the temple so that they can expend every last ounce of energy serving their God. They have determined that they will "waste and wear out their lives" (D&C 123:13) in extending the blessings of the Restoration to people they've never seen before.

It may take a physical toll, but it is invigorating their spirits.

All of this sacrifice takes place in order to help us understand the importance of moving people through the veil. The presence of a veil in the temple is common knowledge. It's similar to the veil that was found in the tabernacle and in other Jewish-built temples. In these ancient temples, no one was allowed to pass through the veil into the Holy of Holies, which symbolized the presence of God. Only the high priest in Israel was allowed to enter on the Day of Atonement. That high priest was representative of Jesus Christ, the only person worthy to enter the presence of God.

I always found it interesting that the very first thing that happened immediately following the death of Christ was that the veil of the Jewish temple was "rent in twain" (Matthew 27:51). The scripture specifies that it was ripped "from the top to the bottom," meaning all the way. Completely.

I'm sure that God didn't pick some random event to happen immediately following the death of His Son. This was an important symbol to each of us that the doors of heaven were opened because of the Atonement. That sign was God's way of telling us that this once-impenetrable barrier that divided us from our Heavenly Father's presence had been obliterated "from the top to the bottom" by the merits and mercy of Christ. It also symbolized that the work for the dead had commenced and that heaven and earth could once again be reunited and sealed through the proxy saving ordinances of the Restoration.

People are going to the temple. There are temple workers galore. Young and old, rich and poor, male and female. These are they "which came out of great tribulation and have washed their robes, and made them white in the blood of the Lamb" in the temple. And there are a lot of us who are engaged in this great latter day reunion that commenced with the subtle appearance of Elijah on April 3, 1836, in the Kirtland temple. More and more people are flocking to the temple because the Spirit urges them. Even more people, both inside and outside of the church are seeking after their ancestors. That same spirit Moroni promised Joseph Smith would be poured out upon the earth under the direction of Elijah is bringing people together for a final gathering, and if it were not so, the earth would be "utterly wasted" at his coming (D&C 2:3).

People Talk . . . but Can't Provide Anything Better

"Let us be articulate, for while our defense of the kingdom may not stir all hearers, the absence of thoughtful response may cause fledglings among the faithful to falter. What we assert may not be accepted, but unasserted convictions soon become deserted convictions."
—*Neal A. Maxwell*[45]

The day I hit the mission field, it was February 5, and the snow was going sideways instead of straight down. Three weeks before that I was surfing Northside Pier in Oceanside, California, wondering how I was going to pull off serving a mission. I never dreamed my first step into the mission field would be into a full blown blizzard.

---

45 Neal A. Maxwell, "All Hell Is Moved," Brigham Young University devotional, November 8, 1977; speeches.byu.edu.

I said to my first companion, "We're going to hang out inside 'til this goes away . . . right?"

"Nah," he said, "Drop your bags and grab your scriptures," and into the storm we went.

The snow eventually stopped but the theological storm raged on. I spent ten and a half months in Grand Rapids, Michigan, home of Calvin College and the Zondervan Press. Without explaining too much, I'll just tell you that this city is not too fond of Mormon missionaries. I was tricked, lured, and almost forced into places with people who were prepared to rip my testimony to shreds. One day while knocking on some doors, a few men invited us to come back to their office. We thought they were interested in hearing our message! Nope! On the contrary—they had a message for me! When I walked into that office, I was shocked. I looked around and saw a Joseph Smith death mask, Kirtland Bank money signed by Joseph Smith, full volumes of the *Journal of Discourses*, *History of the Church*, and almost every video the LDS Church had ever produced. They had current copies of the Ensign and New Era sitting out and marked up. I said, "What the heck do you guys have all this stuff for? Why don't you give it to me?!" I must admit I was jealous of all of their memorabilia. Then they opened up their copies of the Book of Mormon and Doctrine and Covenants, and they had it marked up more than I had seen most active members. I tell you . . . these guys amazed me! I loved it! We had a few laughs at each other's expense and finally got down to the nitty-gritty.

They were kind enough to give me the first word, and away I went with the message of the restored Church. I'm sure they had heard it a million times. It seemed to me as if they were in the crouching position, just waiting to pounce the second I mentioned Joseph Smith . . . and then boom— here it came! The onslaught began with every known claim thrown against the Prophet. "What about this and what about that." These guys were good. They hit him with a left and a right and an upper cut. After a while, I said to them, "Look, everything you've just said, I understand differently and there is really no way for us to agree on the nature of his character because none of us were there to observe him our- selves. So . . . would it be cool if we just left the character of Joseph Smith out of it just this one time and focused on his fruits?" They obliged. (Besides the fact that we had totally different agendas, I actually really liked these guys.)

We left the Book of Mormon out of it as well for the moment and just focused on LDS doctrines as found in the Bible. The discussion was one I'll never forget, and it laid the groundwork for so many discussions I'd have with other people in the future. I attended multiple other churches each week. I'd go to everything from large non-denomina- tional mega churches to small Pentecostal churches. I'd go to Catholic mass on one corner and Lutheran mass on the other. Many times I could visit four churches without even leaving an intersection. (We did this many times to get out of the bitter Michigan cold.) I met with Christians and their pastors on a daily basis and the discussions went much the same as the one I described from above. We talked, they'd pray for my soul, we'd shake hands, and we'd wish each other a happy day.

After talking to all of these wonderful people and witnessing all of the prayers on my behalf, I was left with one outstanding and prominent question in my mind: can anyone give me something better than the Mormon Church? I've been told I'm part of a cult or that Joseph Smith was lazy and indolent or that I don't worship the correct Jesus . . . but never had anyone offered me a better understanding of God or a logical explanation of various key passages found within the same Bible that sat upon their nightstands. I could walk into four different churches on one intersection and not one of them even would attempt to show me that they are the church Christ established when He was on the earth. Isn't that the church you would want to be part of?

What does that church even look like, and is there anyone that can offer any similarities to that ancient Christian church found in the New Testament?

Christ's Church was a living church, meaning it was led by Christ Himself through revelation. When a prophet or apostle got out of line, Christ put him back on track! (See Acts 10:10–16.)

The Church was built upon apostles and prophets (see Ephesians 2:19–20), but I've never had anyone tell me of another church with apostles and prophets. The Bible says we'd have apostles and prophets "until we all came to a unity of faith" (Ephesians 4:11–14). Does it look like we're united?

When Judas was gone, the apostles chose someone to take his spot as an apostle. Did someone authorize the discontinuance of that practice? (See Acts 1:22–25.)

In addition to twelve apostles, Christ also had a body of administrators called the "seventy" (see Luke 10). Is there any other church on the planet that has not only a quorum of twelve but the office of seventy? If that wasn't enough, He also sent them out "two by two" (Mark 6:7). Sound familiar?

There were bishops, elders, pastors, deacons, patriarchs, and most certainly some sort of identifiable priesthood power that was not up for sale or available at a local university. (See Acts 8, 1 Timothy 3, Titus 1:7, Acts 14:23, Titus 1:5, Philippians 1:1.) Degrees don't buy keys, if you will. Christ chose men—they didn't choose Him. (See John 15:16.) They had jobs that provided a livelihood making each of them volunteers. Just your average humble fisherman or tentmaker. Layman at their core.

The name of Christ's Church should be named after Him, right? Doesn't that make sense? Tad Callister once said, "It has always seemed miraculous to me that the Reformation had been in existence for over 300 years before the time of Joseph Smith and no one thought to name his church after Jesus Christ. Of course, since the time of Joseph Smith, others have followed suit, but in some marvelous way the Lord preserved the use of His name until the time of Joseph Smith and the Restoration of Christ's Church."[46]

---

46 Tad R. Callister, "What Is the Blueprint of Christ's Church?" Church Educational System Devotional for young adults, January, 12, 2014.

Christ was literally resurrected and has a body of flesh and bone, according to Luke 24:36–39. To drive the point home, Christ in effect said, "Gimmie some fish," so that He could prove His body was real. Reason leads us to believe that Heavenly Father would also have a body of flesh and bones if Christ said, "The Son can do nothing of himself, but what he seeth the Father do" (John 5:19). To deny it is to deny the purpose of Christ's mission.

The Father and the Son are separate and distinct individuals. Christ exclaimed, "My Father is greater than I," (John 14:28) on one occasion, and on another He looked to heaven and said, "Father, I thank thee that thou hast heard me" (John 11:41). In His last moments on the cross, He asked His Father why He had forsaken Him (see Matthew 27:46). Why on earth in this hour of extreme pain and fatigue would He ask Himself why He has forsaken Himself? He also asks His Father to "forgive them; for they know not what they do" and finally relents, "Into Thy hands I commend my Spirit" (Luke 23:34, 46). To think that Christ is speaking to Himself or some distant manifestation of Himself just doesn't do justice to the character of Christ. The water-gas-ice or 3-in-1 egg examples used to define the Trinitarian concept of God doesn't hold up and is nowhere to be found in the New Testament.

Never in the Bible does it mention children being baptized, and never is baptism performed without an accompanying large body of water. The children were blessed and baptisms were done by immersion in the New Testament.

What church on earth has an answer for children that have died in infancy or those who have never heard the name of Christ? If belief in Christ and baptism by immersion is a requirement for salvation, then there ought to be a provision made by a just and loving God. Peter taught that the gospel was preached to them that are dead (see 1 Peter 4:6) and it follows that Christ's Church would perform baptisms for the dead or for those who didn't have the opportunity to be baptized (see 1 Corinthians 15:29).

What about degrees of glory in heaven or multiple kingdoms? Paul said he visited or saw in vision a "third heaven" (2 Corinthians 12:2–4). Does that mean there is a first and second? What church today talks about these things?

What about eternal marriage? Why would you want to be with your sweetheart "until death do you part" when Paul says that the man and the woman are together "in the Lord" (1 Corinthians 11:11)?

What church echoes Paul's teachings about the body being a temple (see 1 Corinthians 3:16–17) more so than the Mormon Church and its Word of Wisdom? Studies have confirmed that Mormons are among the healthiest people in the world because of this code of living.

Friends have asked me to leave the Church I have described above. But honestly . . . where am I going to learn about all of these things found within the Bible that no one else is talking about? But people say the temple is weird and Joseph Smith was bad and some strange practices have taken place in the past and in the present. That's what they said of Peter and the apostles when they walked the earth. Can you imagine what the Lord taught the Twelve Apostles during His "40-day ministry" when He taught them "things pertaining to the kingdom of god" (Acts 1:13)? Does anyone know what those things were that He taught and why it took 40 days to discuss?

My question is simple and honest: can anyone give me something better than the Mormon Church? And if so, what is it, and how does it stack up against the structure of the original Christian Church that Christ established?

Throwing the Book out the Window

*"He that answereth a matter before he
heareth it, it is folly and shame unto him."*
—*Proverbs 18:13*

About twelve years ago, while serving a mission, I simultaneously had one of the coolest experiences and worst experiences of my life. Both of these experiences took place within about twenty seconds of each other. My companion and I were in our car, sitting at a stop light in Michigan. We saw some people in the car next to us looking our way, and like any good missionaries, we took it as an opportunity to attempt to get the Book of Mormon into their hands.

We started making hand gestures, pointing to the Book of Mormon and asking if they'd be willing to give it a read. They seemed interested, and so with outstretched hands, we successfully completed a mobile hand-off of the Book of Mormon as the cars were all taking off. My companion and I were freaking out with excitement. We couldn't believe that we'd just placed a Book of Mormon (which is a hard thing to do in Michigan, by the way) without even getting out of the car.

We kept on driving down that same road, happy as can be, to our next appointment. We eventually came to a stop light at the next intersection down from where we performed this Book of Mormon hand-off. As the light turned green again, a few cars flew by us, and we also began to move. But as we began to move forward, we heard this massive thud hit the window. Bam! It was loud! We didn't know if we were being shot at or what, but we jumped out of our seats. We saw a blue object slide down the side of the car . . . and then we knew. Those Michiganders to whom we just previously handed off a thousand years of sacred scripture just chucked it back at us in the middle of a busy intersection. We went from elated missionaries to dejected missionaries.

So we pulled over to chill out and consider what had just happened. And in the distance, there was that Book of Mormon being smashed, run over, and desecrated over and over again by each car that cruised on by. We couldn't leave it. We just felt bad. So we waited until the traffic stopped and ran out into the middle of the street and rescued it. When we picked it up, it was in bad shape. Bent, dirty, and permanent tire tracks caused us to call this book "The Wounded Soldier."

We took the book back to our apartment and retired him on the shelf for future missionaries to behold.

Those people who chucked the Book of Mormon out the window that day probably did so ignorantly. We weren't mad at them. We were just sad. They had probably heard something really bad about the Mormons while they were in church or on the internet and decided that the book they were holding in their car was nothing but garbage to be tossed out the window.

When someone slams or disrespects the Book of Mormon, it doesn't do any good to be mad about it. The best thing we can do is calmly share the substantial evidence of its authenticity while giving a personal testimony of the effect the book has had on our own lives. The Book of Mormon will speak for itself when the person studying it does so with an open heart. But until then, the key is to provide a logical case for the Book of Mormon in order to help open their hearts and brains to the remote possibility that it could be true. Those who have written it off prematurely have done so because of worldly hype and nothing else. If only I had the opportunity to talk with those drive-by Book of Mormon chuckers so that I could have properly explained what it was they were actually throwing out the window. If I had the chance, I would have explained the following in the hopes that they would have given the book a chance:

- The book they just threw at us has unequivocally made every individual who read it and applied its principles a better man or woman.
- That book has as much or more life wisdom contained within its pages as any other book that has ever existed. Many non-Mormon historians, theologians, and philosophers have conceded that fact.

They just consider Joseph Smith a genius instead of a prophet.

- The book exists, and it was either fraudulently written or truthfully translated. It would take a more far-fetched faith to believe that Joseph Smith could have produced a book that was much more advanced than anything in his time.

- The people who surrounded Joseph Smith were just as skeptical as anyone else in our day. They themselves tried on multiple occasions to determine if there was any fraudulent activity in translating the Book of Mormon. Each of them came away more convinced than ever that Joseph was a prophet.

- If Joseph Smith were smart enough to write the Book of Mormon, as some have suggested, then he would have had no need of a scribe. He would have carried it out on his own in order to minimize any chance of being exposed.

- None of the witnesses of that book ever faltered in their testimony, even in the face of public scrutiny and humiliation.

- The Book of Mormon is not the work of a creative genius. It's not fantasy, and it's not a novel. It's the complex history of a bunch of concerned parents and prophets. You don't just sit down to write something like that, and scientific analysis of the text confirms the fact that there were different ancient writers with different styles of writing.

- In a world that rejects the Bible as fiction, the Book of Mormon reinvigorates belief in the Bible and reinforces belief in the Savior Jesus Christ.

In almost 200 years, no one has been able to logically explain how the book might have come into existence. But there are millions of people throughout the world that gave the Book of Mormon a chance and can tell you without a doubt that it has had a positive impact on their life. For someone who has given the Book of Mormon a careful study, with and open heart—it's too difficult to write off as a fraud.

That day in Michigan, my companion and I had a Book of Mormon literally thrown out the window at us. The tire tracks across the bent front cover of that book will forever remind me that there are people out there who could really use the teachings found within the same book they chucked at us.

Joseph Smith wrote from Liberty Jail in March of 1839 that we should "waste and wear out our lives in bringing to light all the hidden things of darkness, wherein we know them; and they are truly manifest from heaven" (D&C 123:13). About two weeks later, Joseph was released from Liberty Jail on April 6. Go figure. April 6. Think he could have orchestrated that, too?

The Book of Mormon is a miracle in and of itself, but it's just the tip of the iceberg in this ongoing Restoration on the earth in our days. All a person needs to do is give the Book of Mormon a chance. That's just the starting point . . . and doing so will open up a whole new world of wonder and possibility.

The Book Will Speak for Itself

*"Truth shall spring out of the earth; and
righteousness shall look down from heaven."*
—Psalm 85:11

The Book of Mormon has always spoken for itself. If logically analyzed by sincere truth seekers, it will be hard to deny. I can still remember the exact spot I was sitting when I felt the distinct impression that the Book of Mormon was true. I was on a beach chair on my balcony in Corona Del Mar, California, waiting to go surfing. I had just recently started a serious investigation of the Church when I first began reading the Book of Mormon. As I began my study, I realized that the most important thing I could do is find out whether or not the Book of Mormon was true. People who oppose the Church hate when someone says, "I know the Book of Mormon is true," but I don't know how else to say it. I know the Book of Mormon is true. I'm not going to leave it at that, though . . . I'll tell you how I know it's true.

This wasn't something I figured out overnight. For me, I wanted some hard evidence, and it wasn't enough for someone else to tell me it was true. The existence of the Book of Mormon had to be logical to me. It had to make sense. When I started looking around, it seemed like there were people everywhere saying that the Book of Mormon was a fraud. Since I knew that validity draws fire, it made me want to read it more and dig deeper into the topic. I noticed that most of the people who condemned the Book of Mormon the loudest had never even read the book. They were taking the word of their pastor or mom or friend and writing off the book for good. It might be the funniest thing in the world to me when someone tells me with absolute certainty that the Book of Mormon isn't true after having admitted never actually reading the book themselves.

Here is the bottom line: if the Book of Mormon is true, then Joseph Smith was a prophet. If Joseph Smith was a prophet, then The Church of Jesus Christ of Latter-day Saints is the same Church that Christ established while He was on the earth. It's as simple as that. So the question of all questions deals with the truthfulness of Book of Mormon. All of the other issues that come up are only worth talking about if the Book of Mormon is true, which is why I can't figure out why so many people spend so much time criticizing all of the other aspects or doctrines of the Church.

If you're going to attack something, let's get to the core of it and attack the Book of Mormon. Cut off the head and the body will die, right? Knock down the keystone and the structure comes tumbling down.

One of my friends and a convert to the Church said something I'll never forget. In no way did he mean any disrespect to the Book of Mormon when he said it. He was talking about different times in his life when his faith had been challenged and the role that the Book of Mormon played in his life. He said, with a smile on his face, "If you were to drop a nuclear bomb on my testimony, the Book of Mormon would be like the little cockroach that climbs its way to the surface from beneath all the rubble." One cannot deny the existence of that book. It is there for all to read, and it survives any and every attack.

If you're ever having doubts about the Restoration or about Joseph Smith, just read the Book of Mormon and ask yourself these eleven questions:

1. Could an uneducated boy come up with 531 pages of ancient scripture on his own that was historically accurate and prophetic in nature?

2. Would it be possible for that boy to understand and include ancient Hebrew literary writing devices such as idioms and chiasmus, some of which weren't even discovered until long after Joseph Smith was gone?

3. How would Joseph Smith have been able to know so much about the Middle East, especially the Arabian Peninsula, where Lehi and his family traveled? The book includes findings in that region that no one had discovered yet.

4. How could Joseph Smith come up with roughly 200 new names in the Book of Mormon and then have them turn out to be Semitic in nature?

5. If you think Joseph Smith couldn't have written this book, then where did it come from? If the devil put him up to it . . . then why would Satan want to publish another testament of Jesus Christ, a book that does nothing but promote righteousness? Jesus said that a house divided against itself would fall (Matthew 12:25).

6. Who were the "other sheep" that would hear Jesus's voice, mentioned in John 10:16?

7. Why are there volumes of books written by non-LDS authors[47] stating that Christ came and visited the America's a couple thousand years ago just like it says in 3 Nephi? How would Joseph Smith have known this when, at the time, no one even considered it?

8. If we have the stick of Judah (record of the Jews or the Bible), then where is the stick of Joseph that is referenced in Ezekiel 37:15–20? The Book of Mormon is the only explanation for this scripture. Lehi was a descendant of Joseph—think Joseph Smith could have gotten that right by sheer chance?

9. Of the many witnesses of the Book of Mormon and the gold plates, why would they never deny their testimonies, even when some of them became

47 For example, see L. Taylor Hansen, *He Walked the Americas* (Amherst: Amherst Press, 1963).

bitter toward Joseph Smith? With so many people involved . . . a hoax of this magnitude could never go uncovered.

10. How could the Book of Mormon never contradict itself while being an extremely complex book? After all these years, surely someone would have found something truly contradictory, but they haven't.

And the most important question to ask yourself is, "How do I feel while I read the Book of Mormon?"

Don't let anyone tell you that you can't trust your feelings. We are spiritual beings, and if we can't trust our feelings, then what do we have? Over and over again in the Old and New Testament we're told that we can trust that "still small voice" to guide us in our decisions (1 Kings 19:12). I can write evidence after evidence to back up the Book of Mormon, but each of those evidences I found were only secondary to the whispering of the Spirit I felt that day before I began waxing up my surf board.

Very few people truly know what is buried in those pages of the Book of Mormon. I can't imagine what my life would be like if I had not taken the time to read those pages in between surf sessions as a 21-year-old punk. I can't imagine all of the things I would have missed. I never could have imagined that this book would have an everyday application to my life.

The very first verse in that book opens up by talking about the importance of good parenting. Go figure. As if that's not needed in our day more than ever. That verse wasn't even supposed to appear in the book as the first verse, and yet through a series of events, it landed as the first verse of the entire book.

As I read further, I learned of this guy named Nephi who was completely obedient to his parents. He honored them and supported them. But we live in a day where kids rule over parents and disrespect adults.

Just the other day, I had to act as security for a swim meet to protect an area from kids entering into it. As one kid tried to enter the area, I nicely let him know that this area was closed. He ignored me at first and then got in my face and said, "Don't ever talk smack to me again." This 11-year-old kid might be completely different if he'd learned from Nephi instead of his favorite pop star or TV show. I hope he reads the Book of Mormon someday.

Personally, I learned from Nephi that I need to hold on to the scriptures and keep them close, that doing so will lead me through thick fog and loud voices to the tree (which is Christ), and that once I've partaken of the fruit of Christ's love, that I should never drop that fruit. (See 1 Nephi 8.)

I learned that "the guilty taketh the truth be hard" (1 Nephi 16:2) and that "by small means the Lord can bring about great things" (1 Nephi 16:29). I learned that God doesn't remove trials from my life but that if I keep the commandments, He'll nourish me, and strengthen me, and provide means whereby I can accomplish the things I'm supposed to accomplish (1 Nephi 17:3).

I learned that this great land was chosen to be a land of freedom and that the only thing that can bring that freedom down is the overwhelming voice of the majority choosing wickedness instead of righteousness (Mosiah 29:26–27).

I learned that there is most definitely opposition in all things but that each of us are ultimately here on this earth to experience joy (2 Nephi 2:25).

I learned that through our agency, we choose liberty or captivity being free to act for ourselves. These choices are what make us happy or miserable (2 Nephi 10:23).

I learned that Jesus not only atoned for my sins, but that he took upon himself every mental, emotional, and physical issue I've ever experienced (Alma 7:11–13).

I learned that it's good to be "learned" and smart and approach things intellectually . . . but only if I am also keeping the commandments of God (2 Nephi 9:29).

I learned from Nephi's little brother Jacob to never let "treasure" become my God (2 Nephi 9:30). That if I'm going to seek after riches in this life, I should seek them with the intent to do good for others. What good is an accumulation of wealth if it's not to bless others through that abundance? To not bless others through our abundance is to do the exact opposite of what God does for each of us by blessing us with His abundance.

I learned that about a thousand years of tedious and laborious etching in metal plates had one underlying motivation: "that our children may know to what source they may look for a remission of their sins" (2 Nephi 25:26).

I learned that there would be priestcraft established for the purpose of getting gain through the means of customizing Christ to fit the lifestyles of the day (1 Nephi 22:23).

I learned that the only way I'll ever really be able to get to know Christ and speak with the tongues of angels is to "feast upon" His words (2 Nephi 32:3). I learned that when I don't feel like praying . . . that's when I should pray more "and not faint" (2 Nephi 32:9).

I learned that there is no way in my mind that Joseph Smith came up with 77 long verses of complex allegorical olive tree horticulture out of thin air (see Jacob 5).

I learned from a king named Benjamin that good leaders are always serving others first. That by serving others, we are actually serving God (see Mosiah 2:17–18).

I learned from Abinadi that it's not all that easy to be a disciple of Christ. A guy that was a little caught up in the world named Alma learned that same lesson from Abinadi, and it changed his life. I learned from Alma's son, years later, that even if you haven't been that great of a person in the past, that the power of Christ is able to change your nature and that it's never too late to come back. That even bad dudes can become giants in the kingdom.

I learned that once you've had the gospel change your heart, you immediately have a desire is to reach out and share that knowledge with others . . . even your enemies (see Mosiah 28:3).

I learned from a few repentant soldiers (friends of Ammon) and a bunch of faithful mothers that through the keeping of their covenants, 2,000 of the most righteous youth this world has ever seen were able to confidently fight the battles of the future (see Alma 56:56).

I learned from a guy named Shiblon that it doesn't matter where you serve but how you serve. That there are "Shiblons" everywhere who are "high-yield, low-maintenance members of the Church."[48] Shiblon taught me that you can lead from anywhere and that stability, reliability, and consistency are some of God's most important attributes.

I learned from the actions of a spiritually immature boy named Corianton that "wickedness never was happiness" and that your actions, good or bad, could affect generations to come (Alma 41:10).

I learned from a great captain named Moroni that we should always be prepared. That we should recognize and fortify our "places of weakness" because that's where the enemy will strike (Alma 48:9).

I learned that Christ came to this continent once and that He's on His way back, and that I should be humble as I anticipate His return. If I'm humble, I'm promised that weak things will become strong for me (see Ether 12:27).

I learned in this book that these prophets "saw our day," and now, having read it, I know that they must have been telling the truth.

At the end of this book, I learned that in a world of chaos, I can pray to ask God for answers to the questions of my soul (see Moroni 9:4–5).

But one of the things I learned most of all is that "our lives passed away as it were unto us a dream" (Jacob 7:26). I cannot believe how fast my life has gone by. I was a child

48 Neal A. Maxwell, "The Holy Ghost: Glorifying Christ," *Enisgn*, July 2002.

. . . and now I'm old. The time goes by, and you hope you've been good for something in this world—as did the people who wrote in this book.

These are some of the things I would have missed if I hadn't given the Book of Mormon a fair shake. I haven't even scratched the surface of what I've really learned from this book. I've read lots of books. But never have I seen one book contain such an endless supply of wisdom as I do in this book.

Regardless of whether or not someone chooses to be a member of the Church that produces this book, I hope that every single person on this earth will read it at least one time. It might change your life as it did mine.

If you've never read the book in its entirety, then read it. If it's what it purports to be, then it might just be the most important book you ever read. In my mind, it would be more of a stretch to believe that Joseph Smith could pull this thing off without divine help than to believe that God preserved a record to come forth in the last days. In fact, it would just be flat-out impossible because of the many things Joseph got right, things that had never even been discovered in his time. You just don't pull that off without assistance from above.

There is no doubt those plates existed. Too many people felt them with their own hands and saw them with their own eyes. Even the people who were trying to steal them from Joseph knew that he had something special. They existed, and now you can hold it in your hand and find out for yourself if it's true.

I want my witness to be that of Elder Holland's. "I want it absolutely clear when I stand before the judgment bar of God that I declared to the world . . . that the Book of Mormon is true."[49] The Book of Mormon will speak for itself, but we can speak on behalf of the Book of Mormon and every day become advocates of the eternal truths contained therein.

---

49 Jeffrey R. Holland, "Safety for the Soul," *Ensign*, November 2009.

The Bible Needed to Be Rescued

"In the mouth of two or three
witnesses shall every word be established"
—2 Corinthians 13:1

The Bible is an amazing book . . . as long as people will see it for what it is and what it's not. The Bible is certainly not infallible, and it's definitely not complete. Anyone who tells you that just doesn't understand where the Bible came from and what it went through in order to reach us.

The Bible has stood alone for many years, but in the last days, it's becoming evident why the Bible needs the Book of Mormon.

The Bible is, by definition, a "collection of books" written by various authors who were not always eyewitnesses to the events that they recorded. It was recorded by apostles and disciples many years after the events took place. In some situations, no one was even present to become an eyewitness

145

and thereby had to be given the knowledge of the event by revelation. This fact alone proves that Joseph Smith was not way off base in claiming revelation for various events such as those described in the book of Moses and the book of Abraham.

Take, for instance, the most important event in the history of the world and the climax of all events in the Bible: the Atonement. It took place in the Garden of Gethsemane, and although Peter, James, and John went with Jesus to Gethsemane, they stopped a stone's throw away and subsequently fell asleep. They didn't witness blood coming from every pore, the pleadings of Christ with the Father, or the angel that strengthened Him while He was in pain. Therefore, that event had to have been revealed to someone through revelation in order for it to be recorded in the Gospels.

So, when someone says the Bible is complete, my question is, where did they get that from? Who said that God was going to stop talking to us through prophets? Why would He? He's been doing it since the day He dropped a garden in Eden . . . so why would He stop now when we need it the most?

As you read the Bible—if you get deep enough into it—you'll start to realize that there are some very serious unanswered questions. But if you read the Book of Mormon, in connection with the Bible, you'll start to realize that those questions begin to be answered. In many cases, the Bible tells us what happened, while the Book of Mormon tells us why it happened.

One day I met with a man in Michigan who was a junior pastor for his local congregation. He loved meeting with us, and we with him. He was a very nice and respectful guy and super interested in what we had to say. One day we shared a message with him that included some teachings about the Fall. The next time we came over to his house to meet with him, he told us that he taught his congregation about the Fall out of 2 Nephi 2 in the Book of Mormon . . . but didn't tell them where he had learned the things he was teaching. He conceded to us that 2 Nephi Chapter 2 was the best explanation of the Fall that he had ever heard (and the guy had a library like I had seldom seen),

This guy and his congregation were introduced to the "what" of the Fall in the Bible but were transformed by the "why" of the Fall as explained in the Book of Mormon.

The title page to the Book of Mormon (which was actually the last thing Moroni wrote before he buried the plates) states that the purpose of the Book of Mormon is to "the convincing of the Jew and Gentile that Jesus is the Christ" in the last days. It was sent as another witness of Christ in a day when people are discarding the Bible and leaving Christ for atheism or agnosticism.

Many people cite leaving Christianity due to a lack of evidence in biblical stories and traditions. So the Book of Mormon comes on to the scene and says, "Wait a minute . . . I've got something to say." For over 500 pages, the Book of Mormon goes on to testify of the Bible and of Christ. Literally. Christ is referenced on 95% of the pages in the Book of Mormon, which makes Elder Holland's great-grandfather look pretty wise when he said "no wicked man could write such a book as this; and no good man would write it, unless it were true and he were commanded of God to do so."[50]

---

50 Jeffrey R. Holland, "Safety for the Soul," *Ensign*, November 2009.

Looking for Just One Reason to Believe

"And he shall turn the heart of the fathers to the children, and the heart of the children to their fathers."
—*Malachi 4:6*

There are a lot of reasons why I love the LDS Church, but there's one concept in particular that I love more than any other. This one concept that I've fallen in love with in Mormonism is foreign to all other Christian churches and religions. This concept is doctrinally denounced by the Christian leaders of the world. Pastors and priests don't teach it at all. In fact, they teach against it based on their traditions and understanding of the scriptures. But I learned by experience that this concept, this doctrine, this truth, is burning bright in the hearts of those people who attend those churches.

When I was about ten years old, I got dressed up in white clothes and went to an LDS temple. I had no idea what I was doing. My family entered into this big beautiful building and walked through the halls. I don't remember a lot of the details, but I remember one thing as if it was yesterday. We entered a room where gigantic mirrors were set up on walls directly across from one another. We knelt on some cushions with an altar in the middle of us, and a man in white made some promises to us. When we stood, the man asked me to look into the mirrors and asked me to describe what I was seeing. All these years later, I don't remember how I answered him, but I do remember what I saw and what I felt. I saw my family—together—extending for what looked like an eternity in those mirrors.

That day, I was "sealed" to my parents and my sister with the promise that I could be with them, know them, and love them forever. These people I had been through so much with, and became so close to, weren't going to become angelic strangers when we died. We weren't destined to lose our identities and associations in this life. In fact, these relationships were destined to grow stronger.

This doctrine was sweet to me . . . even at such a young age. Even before I knew it was a doctrine. It was a spiritual knowledge that I knew in my heart was true without yet understanding it intellectually. I never realized that this doctrine was unique to Mormonism. I never realized that pastors and priests from other denominations would preach from their pulpits, telling their members that there would be no marriage, no families, and no identity in the next life. I never realized that many religions banished little children or ignorant grandparents to eternal hell because of the time period in which they lived.

For me, immediate, extended, and adopted families were the very fabric of our existence, both in heaven and on earth. So it was hard to believe that Christianity as a whole was rejecting the idea and hope of a perpetual family.

It wasn't until I started personally knocking on doors in the bitter Michigan cold that I realized that most people don't believe what their pastors are telling them about the family. Over and over again, I would knock on a door, my jaw almost frozen shut, and in the off chance someone opened the door, I'd ask them for the opportunity to share a message with them about families.

Time and time again, people of different denominations would tell me they "already believed in their hearts" that they would be with and know their families in the eternities. Regardless of what their pastor taught regarding the cessation of marriage and family in heaven—for them, they couldn't envision a place being heaven without their families. It was a concept that burned within their hearts. Even though they still attended their church, and still revered their pastor, they were unwilling to surrender the burning within them that told them they have a family in heaven.

I think people would fall in love with the LDS Church if they realized just how similar its teachings are to what they already believe in their hearts. The end game of the entire Church is sealing families. It was never about Joseph Smith or the Book of Mormon or the appearance of Peter, James, and John on the banks of the Susquehanna. Yes, those are super important historical details that undergird the Restoration of the gospel, but all of that always was and always will be about families being together on earth and in heaven through the binding power of the Atonement of Jesus Christ. All of the other important people, places, and pieces of the Restoration existed to do just one thing: preserve, protect, bind, and seal the family together *forever*.

HEAVEN

HELL

Liberal Conservatives

Mormons, liberal?! Are you kidding? "Liberal" is not usually a word that is used to describe Mormons or their theology. Many look at members of The Church of Jesus Christ of Latter-day Saints as ultra conservative, exclusive, and secretive. As a missionary, I had many people exhibit anger toward me, saying that "Mormons believe that they are the only ones who will be saved." In reality, that statement could not be farther from the truth, and I feel like we've got to do a better job at articulating the all-encompassing beauty of the plan of salvation.

With the exception of a few very evil people called the sons of perdition, Mormons believe that every single human being will be saved. They espouse the words of Paul to the Corinthians when he said, "As in Adam all die, even so in Christ shall ALL be made alive" (1 Corinthians 15:22; emphasis added).

That means bad people, good people, and indifferent people will be saved to one degree or another. When I say, "to one degree or another," I mean "one degree or another." Mormons believe that we are all "judged . . . according to [our] works" (Revelation 20:12), and based on that judgment, we'll be sent to a place that God has prepared for us. Jesus spoke of this when he said that there were many mansions in heaven and that he's preparing a place for us (see John 14:2). The Greek word from which "mansions" is derived denotes a place to stay or the place in which one will eventually reside. Paul described those varying degrees of glory as the glory of the moon, the stars, and the sun (see 1 Corinthians 15:40–42) and talked about a man he knew in Christ who was caught up to a "third" heaven (2 Corinthians 12:2–4). If there is a third heaven according to Paul, then there must be first and second heavens as well.

Mormons don't believe in the classic mainstream belief in one heaven and one hell, and as far as I'm concerned, Mormonism has a more liberal theology on salvation than any religion I've studied. We don't believe that if Johnny committed one more sin than Cyndi, and both were on the dividing line between heaven and hell, that Johnny is eternally cast off and Cyndi enjoys eternal bliss. Mormons believe that even those who don't confess the name of Christ will be saved. That's crazy talk in an evangelical world. Even those wayward children of bishops that went to church their whole life but decided to turn away from the Church and from Christ. Saved. Even more crazy right?! They will be "saved," yet they will need to pay the price for their own sins, rendering the Atonement of Christ partially ineffective in their lives. How about the heathen that grew up never ever hearing the name "Jesus Christ"? Damned? No! Saved? Yes! Why? Because Christ's resurrection is universal. What about Christ saying that you must confess His name and be baptized to be saved? The heathen didn't do either. (See 1 Corinthians 15:29; 1 Peter 4:6; and 1 Peter 3:18–19.)

Mormons, by and large, are striving to attain the "glory of the sun," or the "third" heaven spoken of by Paul. In doing so, they claim no exclusivity on this degree of glory. They want all to be there—which is why they zealously trade in their material lives and comfy college lives for a nerdy little helmet and a mountain bike. However, if someone chooses not to worry about it, Mormons believe that Christ "has prepared a place" for them also, and they will be comfortable and happy about it. In fact, it will be glorious.

The Prophet Joseph Smith is quoted as saying, "Our Heavenly Father is more liberal in His views, and boundless in His mercies and blessings, than we are ready to believe or receive."[51] In reality, Mormons are the most conservative *and* liberal people that I know. They are trying to conserve

---

51 Joseph Smith, as quoted in *Teachings of the Prophet Joseph Smith*, sel. Joseph Fielding Smith (Salt Lake City: Deseret Book, 1976), 257.

primitive Christianity, true doctrine, and family values. But when you get into the doctrine, you find the most liberal and accepting views of any other Christian denomination. It's the blend of conservative and liberal doctrine that makes Mormonism so appealing to me.

Pageantry Gives
Way to Teaching

"A good teacher is like a candle—it
consumes itself to light the way for others."
—Mustafa Kemal Atatürk[52]

I know we're not supposed to rank callings in the Church, but I've got to do it here. I think I'll be justified in this case, seeing as that Paul does the ranking for me when he's addressing the Corinthians. Have you ever asked someone what their calling was and noticed the difference in their reply depending on the perceived importance of that calling?

"Oh, yeah . . . well, I'm just a Sunday School teacher . . . not much to it. No big deal."

Funny, that same person invited an entire posse to come and watch him take the stand when he was called in to

---

52 Quote is commonly attributed to Atatürk and is purportedly translated from the original Turkish, though the translation has not been formally published in English.

the bishopric a few years back. "Congratulations, Brother So-and-so. . . ."

Why are administrative callings sometimes treated as a public inauguration, but the ever important calling to teach the 14- and 15-year-olds is met with indifference? Why the lack of back-slapping for that new calling to teach the temple prep class? It's a cultural thing . . . with no doctrinal justifications. The scriptures paint an entirely different picture of the importance of teachers.

Let me go back to Paul. "God hath set some in the church, first apostles, secondarily prophets, thirdly teachers, after that miracles" (1 Corinthians 12:28). Elder McConkie said to

> Note the order of propriety. In the true Church apostles are first; they hold the keys of the kingdom, receive revelation for the Church, and regulate all of its affairs in all the world as they are guided by the power of the Holy Ghost. . . . Next to the apostles stand the prophets, every prophet ministering in his own place and sphere. . . . After apostles and prophets come teachers. Every teacher is expected to be a prophet and to know for himself of the truth and divinity of the work. Indeed, in the true sense, a teacher is greater than a prophet, for a teacher not only has the testimony of Jesus himself, but bears that testimony by teaching the gospel.[53]

So why is it that when someone gets called as a gospel teacher, sometimes they begin to slack? Not too long ago

---

53 Bruce R. McConkie, "The Doctrinal Restoration," in *The Joseph Smith Translation: The Restoration of Plain and Precious Truths*, ed. Monte S. Nyman and Robert L. Millet (Provo: Religious Studies Center, Brigham Young University, 1985), 1–22.

I was called to serve as the ward Sunday School president. Some of my friends joked with me that I had just become the official "bell-ringer," "hall-monitor," and "role-keeper." Someone even came up to me and made a joke that the ward Sunday School president was where they called "inactive men to serve in order to make them feel important." We all had some good laughs, and I dropped a few jokes on myself at my own expense in the process as well. No harm intended.

But through all of that, I realized that one of the most serious flaws in our Church culture is the unspoken—and sometimes spoken—devaluation of gospel teachers. Even if it's just in jest, I realized that this feeling of unimportance manifested itself through the level of consistency shown among some of the teachers in their ward callings. It has become quite the regular thing for teachers to call regularly at 10 p.m. on Saturday night to bail on their class the next morning. Sometimes teachers just flat out never show up without letting anyone know. They figure that it's no big deal and that "Brother So-and-so can just put a movie on for the kids." Meanwhile, the kids get used to a bunch of adult, "throwing something together" at the last minute to "keep them busy." But these kids aren't stupid! They know when they're being placated or babysat. Their perception of the importance of their class was based on the consistency and preparation of their teacher.

A couple years ago, I attended a CES training in which a young stake president, who also happened to be an institute director, stood up to give some remarks about the calling to be a teacher. He said something along the lines of, "It's hard for me to call new bishops, but I lose sleep over the responsibility to call a new seminary teacher. You are that important." I loved hearing this!

There is no doubt that administrative positions, such as an elders quorum president, Relief Society president, or bishop, are important—as indicated by this stake president. But think about it. How often does the general population of the ward really and truly interact with those leaders? Many of those callings are focused on the temporal welfare of members of the ward, but the teachers of the ward are literally responsible for the spiritual nourishment of every man, woman, and child in that ward. If the teachers slack, or view their calling as ancillary . . . what do we have? Without dedicated and effective teachers, the general body of the Church would diminish and crumble from a lack of spiritual enthusiasm and doctrinal understanding. We won't need administrative callings if Church members' testimonies don't stay strong.

Consider the seminary teacher who is with the youth every single morning of their high school life. Is there any greater influencer for the youth of this Church than their regular weekday and Sunday teachers? As much as we'd like to hope that parents spend a dedicated forty-five minutes a day in gospel instruction, do you think that is an actual reality? No. Probably not. It would be nice . . . but it's probably not realistic.

The teachers of this Church have a duty, a responsibility, and an opportunity that is unparalleled in this Church.

Sometimes that fact gets lost in the cultural hoopla of other callings and their associated importance. The gospel teacher has got to be on their game, and the rest of the Church has got to back them up and give them the support they need. This is especially true for the teachers of the youth.

There was a day when it was cool to be a master teacher. We should do whatever we can as a Church to make it cool again.

No Bad Teachers

*"If you want to build a ship, don't drum up people together
to collect wood and don't assign them tasks and work, but
rather teach them to long for the endless immensity of the sea."*
—Antoine de Saint-Exupéry[54]

Over the years, I've had the opportunity to sit through some really bad classes and some really good classes during church. The bad classes left me sleepy, somber, and longing to have that hour of my life back. The good classes, on the other hand, inspired me to dig deeper, become better, and try harder in life.

Some might argue that there are just plain ol' bad teachers with subsequently bad classes. Bruce R. McConkie once said:

> We come into these congregations, and sometimes a speaker brings a jug of living water that has in it many gallons. And when he pours it out on the congregation, all the members

54 Antoine de Saint-Exupéry, *Citadelle* (Paris: Gallimard, 1948), 687.

have brought is a single cup and so that's all they take away. Or maybe they have their hands over the cups, and they don't get anything to speak of.

On other occasions we have meetings where the speaker comes and all he brings is a little cup of eternal truth, and the members of the congregation come with a large jug, and all they get in their jugs is the little dribble that came from a man who should have known better and who should have prepared himself and talked from the revelations and spoken by the power of the Holy Spirit.[55]

For the most part, people come to class looking to be edified. Unfortunately, teachers sometimes do things that make it hard for that to happen in their classes.

I don't believe that there are bad teachers. There are only good teachers who slip into bad habits, subsequently annoying their class members. Everyone has something to offer to a classroom as long as they get a few things straight. When class members are annoyed, they stop paying attention or refuse to participate. I've noticed that the following seven things seem to take place in our classes on a regular basis and account for most of the "bad" lessons.

1. Start by Apologizing for a Lack of Preparation

This is the worst way to start your lesson off. Whether you just procrastinated until the last minute or your Sunday school president called you at 10 p.m. on a Saturday night, it makes no difference to the class. All you do by telling them that you're unprepared is give

55 Bruce R. McConkie, "The Seven Deadly Heresies," Brigham Young University devotional, June 1, 1980; speeches.byu.edu.

them a reason to check out early. I know you might be saying it because you want to garner some sympathy from those in the classroom so that they don't think you're an idiot, but announcing this doesn't help your situation. It only impairs it. When you're in a bind for last minute content, focus 100% of your time on crafting some deep and thoughtful questions. You can take 10 minutes, review the content, and jot down the most important thought-provoking questions to ask the class. Then build off of their responses.

2. The Lecture Rant

Speaking of questions, I think it's so funny how so many of us spend hours trying to conjure up a series of grandiose statements for our lessons while completely neglecting to spend time contemplating deep and considerate questions. It should be the other way around. Even when we do have ample time to prepare, we should still spend at least 90% of our time determining the right questions to ask for a lesson. The right questions will stir emotions and elicit thoughtful responses and personal experiences. These questions enable us to be "edified together" rather than listening to one person lecture or rant.

3. Botched Questions

Now that you know how important good questions are, it's maybe just as important to actually ask those questions properly.

Rhetorical questions should be avoided at all costs. I can't count how many times I've been sitting in class, wondering if I should answer the teacher's rhetorical question. Maybe worse than that is when I can't figure out whether the question is rhetorical or not. "You guys think it's important to keep the commandments . . . right?" Silence. Umm . . . yes. Then there's the times when we read paragraph after paragraph, only to have the teacher eventually ask the repetitive, "So what do you think that means?" No one says it, but everyone is thinking to themselves, "Which of the premises did you want me to answer?" Then there's the often-used "guess what I'm thinking" questions. We go round and round until someone gets the right answer. Meanwhile, the fifteen people who got the answer wrong just started checking their phones for Facebook messages and won't be raising their hands the rest of the class—and maybe even for the rest of your tenure as a teacher.

4. The "I Don't Care What You Have to Say" Tick

Have you ever generated the courage to answer a question or share a personal story, only to have the teacher break eye contact with you, look at the clock, or start studying his or her notes? I have. And actually I'd say that this happens on a regular basis. Of everything on this list, it might be the thing that annoys me the most. You know what it tells me? It says to me that what I have to say isn't very important and that you're concerned that my response is going to dig into your lecture time. You're worried that you might not be able to drop that climactic statement on the class that you'd been preparing all night because now, the "time is running out."

Most teachers use the time when people are commenting or responding as "down time" or as an opportunity to look ahead in their lesson and "find their place." There's a good chance that it's not the teacher's intention to offend the commenter. The problem is that this teacher is placing more importance on what he is going to say next instead of truly listening to the comment and building off of it. President Eyring said,

> You may have had the experience I have had of noticing that not very many people during a conversation listen carefully to the other person. Generally they are focusing on what they said last or what they will say next.[56]

Again, it's usually not intentional . . . but it is detrimental.

5. I Have to Cover Everything in the Lesson

Your job as a teacher is not to cover the lesson but to leave people better than you found them in the short time that you're with them. The only way to do that is by building an atmosphere in which the Spirit can operate on people unrestrained. By "trying to cover everything," you're actually suppressing things that the Spirit might have wanted to teach.

---

56 Henry B. Eyring, "Child of Promise," Brigham Young University devotional, May 4, 1986; speeches.byu.edu.

6. No Love for a Fearful Comment

Remember that time you thought you gave a really thoughtful comment and when you were done the teacher just moved on without saying anything at all? It kind of made you feel lame, didn't it? The greatest teachers I know always take the time to acknowledge, appreciate, and build off of others' comments. This behavior encourages more comments and instills confidence in the class members. No one wants to look dumb when they raise their hand. It's the role of a good teacher to ensure that this doesn't happen regardless of what comes out of a person's mouth.

7. No Respecter of Time

So you're teaching Sunday School in the Relief Society room. You think you're on a roll and you're feeling good about yourself. You know your time has come to a close . . . but you really wanted to get to that big spiritual statement you thought of last night. You know, the one that's going to shake the earth with spiritual power. You've just got to get it out before class is over but those pesky class members have been using up all your time. Then, at five minutes after the hour, you drop it on them—and guess what? No one even heard you.

I've heard it said that the Spirit leaves the room when the class is over. That's not doctrine, but it has always felt true to me. When I've run over my allotted time, I can tell the class is not the same. Plus, the Relief Society presidency is giving you the stink eye through the windows on the closed door. In five minutes, you've just turned a potentially good lesson into an irritating one because you had to get to that last statement. It's not worth it. Save it for another time. Make sure that you keep an eye on the time or ask someone in the class to be your "time-keeper" so that you never break this rule.

We've just gone from start to finish in a classic Sunday school class. All of us are teachers in some way and at some time. All of us want to do a good job and facilitate spiritual experiences for others.

Eliminate these seven habits and become a legendary gospel teacher . . . because we'll need you in the coming days, when it becomes harder and harder to endure the trials of being a member of the Church.

Peeling Back Polygamy

"The Latter-day Saints were long regarded as a polygamous people. That plural marriage has been practiced by a limited proportion of the people, under sanction of Church ordinance, has never since the introduction of the system been denied. But that plural marriage is a vital tenet of The Church is not true. What the Latter-day Saints call celestial marriage is characteristic of The Church, and is in very general practice; but of celestial marriage, plurality of wives was an incident never an essential. Yet the two have often been confused in the popular mind."
—James E. Talmage[57]

Fact: Early Mormons practiced polygamy.

Fact: It sounds just as weird to me as it does to you.

Fact: If you're a Christian, Jew, or Muslim, then you'd have to abandon your faith if you condemn periodic requirements to live in polygamous societies.

---

57 James E. Talmage, *The Story of "Mormonism"* (Liverpool: Millennial Star Office, 1907), 86.

Fact: If you're an atheist, then there is no moral law prohibiting you from practicing polygamy. Any moral laws that you live by have either been dictated by society or self. And if we're living by societal norms . . . anything goes, as those can change with the wind.

My wife and I have shied away from D&C 132 for a while now. A surface reading of it just doesn't sit well with most people . . . but the research my wife has put in on this subject over has blown my mind. She went to God in prayer and analyzed every verse in that section. I wanted to get her feelings, her perspective, and her thoughts before I published anything else on this subject.

While my wife was doing her own research, I was busy asking respected friends and knowledgeable Church members (many of whom I would consider scholars) one question: "Do you believe that polygamy is a celestial law that will be required in the celestial kingdom?" The almost unanimous answer was yes.

My immediate follow up question and response was, "Ok . . . so who taught you that?"

A puzzled look always follows as they say, "Well . . . well . . . erm . . . I'm not sure. That's just what I've always heard."

"Heard it where?" I'd ask.

"Well . . . I don't know. That's a good question"

I've been trying to figure out where, how, and why I've been taught that plural marriage is an eternal celestial principle. For the life of me, I can't remember why I think that. Is it just Mormon folklore or something someone extrapolated from the Doctrine and Covenants or some *Journal of Discourses* quotation? Many Mormons will say the same thing, that they've heard plural marriage is an eternal principle. But my question is, where did they hear it? Who taught it? And why do so many Mormons believe it?

Maybe it's time to NOT believe that.

Trying to figure out why Mormons used to practice polygamy is important to a lot of members of the Church. It's been especially difficult for women over the years, which is understandable. Valerie Hudson Cassler and Alma Don Sorensen once wrote that "no woman who has ever felt pain about polygamy is satisfied until her concerns about the hereafter are at least addressed. No woman who has felt pain about polygamy can honestly strive for a place in the celestial kingdom unless she feels that that kingdom is a place in which she would actually want to live."[58]

It's painful enough to think about polygamy in mortality, but to think that it might persist in the eternities is faith-shattering for some people. We've got to acknowledge that fact and discuss it.

The first thing we need to establish is that when you hear something about polygamy from media outlets or even from other members of the Church, you've got to keep in mind that they might not know what they're talking about. Hey! I may not even know what I'm talking about. There are stories, interpretations, and opinions from so many different people that it makes it difficult to know what really happened . . . and why it really happened.

58 Alma Don Sorensen and Valerie Hudson Cassler, *Women in Eternity, Women in Zion* (Springville: Cedar Fort, Inc., 2004), 213.

I don't know what Joseph Smith's motives were. How can anyone know? All I'm saying is that people condemn Joseph Smith for the same things they should be condemning the prophets of the Bible for. No one can know of the intentions of the old prophets, yet we seem to just let them slide because of a "cultural acceptance" in their day. What's wrong is wrong and what's right is right—in any period of time and regardless of culture.

Here's what I believe: Plural marriage is NOT a celestial law, and it's NOT required in the celestial kingdom. It's a temporal, earthly law given as an exception to the spiritual celestial law of monogamy. I feel like it can be proven according to the scriptures.

The Lord rips polygamy in the Book of Mormon. There were a few guys in Book of Mormon times who were trying to take multiple wives, using David and Solomon as justification for their actions.

"For they seek to excuse themselves in committing whoredoms, because of the things which were written concerning David, and Solomon his son. Behold, David and Solomon truly had many wives and concubines, which thing was abominable before me, saith the Lord" (Jacob 2:23–24).

The Lord is stating that having many wives was "abominable" to Him—and yet the Bible is clear that David was justified in having many wives when the Lord spoke through His prophet Nathan to David.

"And *I gave* thee thy master's house, and thy master's wives into thy bosom, and gave thee the house of Israel and of Judah; and if that had been too little, I would moreover have given unto thee such and such things." (2 Samuel 12:8; emphasis added)

God was not condemning polygamy in David's day; He was endorsing it. David only got himself in hot water when he went after Uriah's wife (Bathsheba) and then arranged for Uriah's death to cover up the baby growing in Bathsheba's womb.

Again, in 1 Kings 15:5 it says, "David did that which was right in the eyes of the Lord, and turned not aside from any thing that he commanded him all the days of his life, save only in the matter of Uriah the Hittite."

Polygamy was "right in the eyes of the Lord" and yet simultaneously "abominable" in the sight of Lord.

At first glance it looks like an obvious contradiction between the Bible and the Book of Mormon, but we've got to ask ourselves if there are any other scriptural instances in which God commands or allows mankind to do something temporarily that is otherwise "abominable" to the Lord.

After studying D&C 132 in depth, polygamy, to me, has become less about sex and more about sacrifice. This principle, in all actuality, requires the ultimate emotional sacrifice. To those required to live this principle, this sacrifice was worse than death. The emotional pain surpassed anything they could have suffered physically.

Good men hated it. (Yes, they did.)

Women hated it. (Of course they did.)

Joseph Smith hated it and ran from it. (This he stated over and over again.) Then he told others that it would be one of the most challenging thing the saints would ever face.

It is compared with only one other type of sacrifice in all of scripture: the Abrahamic sacrifice. Why?

Most of us have heard of an Abrahamic sacrifice but few understand what it really means. I had no idea how important understanding this doctrine would be to understanding plural marriage.

The Abrahamic sacrifice has a few significant attributes that set it apart from any other kind of sacrifice.

For some reason, God sometimes requires people to contradict and disobey a general commandment that has been given. For instance, a general commandment that has helped people and civilizations for years has been the commandment "Thou shalt not kill" (Exodus 20:13). To "not kill" is the general law that is calculated to bring happiness for following it in this life. But at times God has required people to break that law in order to follow a temporary law that is an exception to the general law.

Remember when God commanded Israel to go after the Amalekites and "utterly destroy all that they have, and spare them not; but slay both man and woman, infant and suckling, ox and sheep, camel and ass" (1 Samuel 15:3)? Can you imagine how those Israelites felt, as they had been taught their entire lives that they should not kill?

I can't imagine how Nephi must have felt when he was commanded to kill Laban. Nephi said, "Never at any time have I shed the blood of man. And I shrunk and would that I might not slay him" (1 Nephi 4:10). His entire life of righteousness seemed to hang in the balance as he was faced with this decision to break a commandment that he knew was right and good. He "shrunk" at the idea.

And then there's Abraham.

Consider what Abraham was commanded to do to his son Isaac. He was commanded to take his and Sarah's only son Isaac and sacrifice him in cold blood. Imagine the vice that must have crushed Abraham's heart as he was commanded to do this thing. They waited years and years for that kid, and now the Lord commanded Abraham to make this seemingly pointless journey to Mount Moriah. Abraham knew that one of the most severe commandments was "thou shalt not kill," and yet here he was, raising the knife to his pride and joy. It was the most strenuous test of faith.

Something similar happened to Adam and Eve. They were commanded not to partake of the fruit of the tree of knowledge of good and evil, yet at the same time they were commanded to multiply and replenish the earth (Genesis 1:28; 2:17). You can almost feel how painful it was for them to make the decision to partake of the fruit of that tree. They didn't want to disobey. It was a carefully thought-out decision for them to eat that fruit. It wasn't a mistake. They were breaking one commandment and knowingly bringing great pain upon themselves in order to follow another commandment. They broke that commandment so that each of us could come into the world. It was a sacrifice to them, and there was an eventual "escape." That escape consisted of the Savior coming into the world to reverse the effects of the Fall.

Even in the Atonement, we see this principle at work. You can argue that because Christ had power over His own life and could have summoned "legions of angels" to save Him from the Jews (Matthew 26:53), He actually transcended one general commandment in order to keep His Father's exceptional commandment to give His life. It isn't lawful for one to "sacrifice" one's self, but because the Father commanded His innocent Son to give His life, He was justified and did not commit sin in following that command. His "release" or "escape" came on the third day as He was raised from the tomb.

God required these people to follow an exceptional, temporary law in order to accomplish His purposes, even though those purposes were not made known to them at the time. It's the most spiritually excruciating sacrifice anyone can experience. The general commandment brings happiness, and the exceptional commandment brings temporary misery.

I believe that polygamy is one of those exceptional commandments given to men and women at various times for specific purposes. The Lord tells Jacob that He will institute plural marriages for one purpose: "For if I will, saith the Lord of Hosts, raise up seed unto me, I will command my people; otherwise they shall hearken unto these things" (Jacob 2:30).

Between reading this verse and the previous verses in Jacob, it becomes clear that the general law is monogamy.

Monogamy is never restricted in the scriptures, but polygamy is always restricted unless God needs to "raise up" a righteous seed to fulfill His purposes.

Did you know that Christ Himself was descended from a polygamous heritage? The seemingly endless genealogies in the very first chapters of Matthew have always bored me, but then someone pointed out that if you look at the genealogies of Christ, you'll see that He descended from the house of David. The house of David was one of the largest polygamous houses in recorded history. Clearly, God allows polygamy in specific circumstances.

And then we run into D&C 132, where the Lord draws an interesting comparison between Abraham's willingness to sacrifice Isaac and Abraham's willingness to enter into plural marriage. In verse 34, it says that God commanded Abraham to enter into plural marriage. It appears that Abraham was commanded to do this in order to "raise up seed." Sarah was the one who gave Hagar to Abraham and in doing this, Sarah was conforming to the law that was given to Abraham. In this regard, Sarah was enduring an Abrahamic sacrifice of her own. In verse 36, the Lord draws an instant comparison between Abraham being required to offer Isaac and Abraham being willing to enter into plural marriage. In both cases here, the Lord is saying that it "was accounted unto him for righteousness" for being willing to depart from the general law to obey the exceptional law as the Lord commanded it.

Abraham, Sarah, and Hagar did not enjoy the exceptional commandment to create a plural family. The Bible makes that really clear. This was Abraham's first major test to prove that he was willing to do anything that the Lord commanded him. Abraham didn't want to marry Hagar and have a child with her or else he would have done so sooner. He wanted to be married to Sarah and have a child with her, but the Lord prolonged that event in order to test their faith and teach them about sacrifice. As a result of their obedience, they were blessed with Isaac in a miraculous fashion.

Unfortunately, Abraham and Sarah were not yet done being tested. Abraham was once again asked to disobey a general law in order to obey an exceptional law. The Lord told him to take his son Isaac to Mount Moriah, to bind him and sacrifice him. You've got to be kidding, right?!

Abraham goes as far as to raise his knife, and as he does so, the Lord provides an escape. A ram is offered in Isaac's stead, and Abraham's happiness is restored to him.

As we go back into D&C 132, in verse 50 the Lord tells Joseph Smith that He's seen his "sacrifices and obedience to that which" He had commanded him in reference to plural marriage. "Therefore," says the Lord, "I make a way for your escape, as I accepted the offering of Abraham of his son Isaac."

Why does the Lord use the word "escape" here? That means that the sacrifice that is being required of Joseph Smith will come to an end.

Now this is where people may think I'm completely insane for believing such a thing. Most people would never dream or think that a guy would consider marrying multiple women to be a sacrifice, but to a good man who loves his wife, this would indeed be a sacrifice.

If the Lord is calling plural marriage an "Abrahamic sacrifice," then it will bring comfort to someone who has been required to live the law of plural marriage to know that the final attribute of an Abrahamic sacrifice is the eventual release—or an "escape," as the Lord put it.

If plural marriage is a painful sacrifice for all of the good parties involved, then why would the Lord require it to continue in the celestial kingdom? Why would God condemn the practice of plural marriage so strongly, even calling it "abominable," if it was in fact a celestial law? Because based on these scriptures, the "sacrifice" is eventually brought to an end so that happiness can be restored as it was with Abraham.

In no place in the scriptures do I see the Lord eluding to a polygamous requirement in the next life. I see Him condemning it in this life, except at times in which He has needed to raise up seed for His own purposes as a bona fide sacrifice and departure from the general law of monogamy.

Too many people believe that the entire section of D&C 132 is about polygamy and mistakenly attribute the first half (the half about the new and everlasting covenant of eternal marriage) to plural marriage, when in fact the topic of plural marriage is not even discussed until the second half of the revelation. I believe it is eternal marriage (monogamy) that is required in the celestial kingdom, not plural marriage.

But you're probably concerned about all the people being sealed to each other, right?

All of the reasons someone might bring up as a logical reason to practice polygamy in heaven are complete speculation. There is no doctrine about more women being in heaven or there not being enough time to make babies. No doctrine. Actually, most of the explanations aren't even logical.

God promised Joseph Smith an "escape" from that exceptional law—so why would it be required in heaven?

Why this type of thinking continues on in the Church is a mystery to me. Heck, I'm grateful for all the media coverage because it's forced me and my wife to consider this principal carefully and prayerfully.

I think people try to come up with whatever they can think of to rationalize why they might have to practice polygamy in heaven without ever realizing that it might not even be required in heaven after all. They never even consider that it was an exception to the celestial law of monogamy, in which husband and wife look forward to being with one another and only each other in the eternal worlds.

But what about men who have been sealed to more than one woman? Why were Joseph Smith and others sealed to so many women, including a 14-year-old?

Some of the sealings and marriages that took place during the early days of the Church were for assuring familial bonds in eternity and did not involve sex, but then other marriages appear to have taken place in order to "raise up a righteous seed." That raising up a righteous seed portion is where I believe men and women were put to the Abrahamic test. That must have been insanely difficult for men and especially for women. It's understandable that those affected by this principle reacted so harshly to it.

Even Joseph Smith said in a very candid way, "I don't blame any one for not believing my history. If I had not experienced what I have, I would not have believed it myself."[59]

In the early days, the Church was still trying to wrap their heads around sealings. The Restoration took place over time and was difficult to understand. Many of the sealings that took place were done as "proxy" or "stand-in" marriages. You had people being sealed to General Authorities in every direction to assure their exaltation. Sometimes you had widows get sealed to general authorities whose husbands had died before receiving the gospel and then the husband sealed to that same general authority as a child in order to "keep him in the family."[60]

To quote Valerie Hudson Cassler and Alma Don Sorensen:

> Many women [became] plural wives because of the mistaken understanding that they could not be sealed to their dead husbands and could not gain their exaltation unless sealed to someone as a wife. For example, women who had never even met Joseph Smith while he was alive were sealed to him after his death. One woman had her aged mother sealed to her (the daughter's) husband shortly before the mother died so that the mother could receive her exaltation. Wilford Woodruff had over 400 of his dead female ancestors sealed

59 Joseph Smith, in *History of the Church*, 6:317.
60 Gordon Irving, "The Law of Adoption: One Phase of the Development of the Mormon Concept of Salvation, 1830-1900," *BYU Studies*, vol. 14, no. 3 [1974].

to him as wives. These practices seem to indicate that the parties involved understood the man in question was more a proxy so that the woman could receive the marriage ordinance and thus her exaltation, rather than an understanding that these women were married in some meaningful sense to these particular men for all eternity. What can it mean to have a dead woman sealed to you, whom you have never met in this life, whose will on the matter you cannot possibly know, and who is in fact one of your great-great grandmothers? Or to have your own mother-in-law sealed to you as a wife? Or, in the case of a woman, to be sealed to a dead man whom you have never met, and whose will on the matter you cannot possibly know? These marriages make sense best as proxy marriages. Indeed, when President Wilford Woodruff announced in 1894 that women could be sealed to their dead husbands (and children to their dead parents) even if the deceased had not been baptized before their deaths, many thousands of sealing transfers took place to rightfully reorganize family lines.[61]

Cassler and Sorenson also point out that it appears that there is also a doctrine of "transferability." Joseph Fielding Smith mentioned this doctrine as well.

When a man and a woman are married in the temple for time and all eternity and then separate, the children will go with the parent who is justified and who has kept the covenants. If neither of them has kept his covenants, the children may be taken away from both of them and given to somebody else, and that would be by virtue of being born under the covenant. A child is not to be sealed the second time when born

---

61 Alma Don Sorensen and Valerie Hudson Cassler, *Women in Eternity, Women in Zion* (Springville: Cedar Fort, Inc., 2004), 215–216.

under the covenant, but by virtue of that birthright can be transferred.[62]

This appears to be what is happening with all of these sealings. Heavenly Father's goal is to seal every man and woman, from Adam down, back to God. The important seal is that of one being sealed back to God as opposed to the devil sealing you his (Alma 34:35). Once a woman is sealed back to God through the new and everlasting covenant, her ordinance can be transferred to another worthy priesthood holder of her choice. It makes sense. If she doesn't want to enter into a polygamous relationship, there will be someone for her to form a monogamous relationship with and she will be happy. How else could it be?

Someone might say that things will be different in heaven and polygamy might not be a big deal when you get to heaven. That might be true—but if "that same sociality which exists among us here will exist among us there" (D&C 130:2), then many of the saints will not be desirous to live that exceptional law.

Joseph Smith said, "I have constantly said no man shall have but one wife at a time, unless the Lord directs otherwise,"[63] and Bruce R. McConkie said, "According to the Lord's law of marriage, it is lawful that a man have only one

---

62 Joseph Fielding Smith, *Doctrines of Salvation,* 3 vols., edited by Bruce R. McConkie (Salt Lake City: Bookcraft, 1954–1956), 2:91.
63 Joseph Smith, in *History of the Church,* 6:46.

wife at a time, unless by revelation the Lord commands plurality of wives in the new and everlasting covenant."[64]

These quotations reinforce that plural marriage is an "exception commandment" for specific earthly purposes of raising up seed unto God in this life only. In the next life, we'll be in no rush to "raise up seed" because there will be no time constraints.

I'm not saying polygamy cannot exist in the celestial kingdom. I'm just saying that I don't believe that it's required in the celestial kingdom. I don't believe it is the de facto standard in the celestial kingdom or that it will be required or demanded of any exalted individuals. In everything that I read in the scriptures and from the teachings of the prophets and general authorities, I see the teaching that if one man and one woman enter into the new and everlasting covenant of marriage, they have the opportunity to receive their exaltation. Nowhere does it say that I am required to take another wife for exaltation. I believe a husband and wife can rest assured that if they prefer, they are perfectly justified living the eternal and generally acceptable law of monogamy.

That brings comfort to me. It brings comfort to my wife. I hope it brings comfort to you.

What I have written here is my opinion. It's not official doctrine, and I don't speak on behalf of the Church. I love the Church and am grateful for the Church. My only goal in writing this is to help those who might be struggling with

64 Bruce R. McConkie, *Mormon Doctrine*, 2d ed., (Salt Lake City: Bookcraft, 1966), 577.

this topic to consider every angle before becoming irritated or depressed about the subject.

I'm sure someone will find some sort of quote to try and prove me wrong or something. That's all right! Like I said, I may be wrong. I'm like you, seeking to learn, seeking to grow. I love to see different angles, and I'm happy to always consider additional light and knowledge, even if it contradicts what I believe. I don't know every single quote that was ever made on the subject. All I know is that I've found peace through my recent studies and that those studies appear to jive with the scriptures.

For the Church's official releases on the subject you can visit https://www.lds.org/topics/plural–marriage–and –families–in–early–utah?lang=eng and https://www.lds.org/ topics/plural–marriage–in–kirtland–and–nauvoo?lang=eng and https://www.lds.org/topics/plural–marriage–in–the –church–of–jesus–christ–of–latter–day–saints?lang=eng.

You should also read *Women in Eternity, Women of Zion* by Alma Don Sorensen and Valerie Hudson Cassler. This book contains some of the best explanations on the subject that I've seen yet and is the source from which we were able to see the connection between Abrahamic sacrifice and polygamy. This find was a hidden gem to us.

I believe in my heart that polygamy is a temporal exception to the general and eternal law of monogamy. This exception was in play in the Old Testament and in the early days of the LDS Church. It was a sacrifice to those involved, and in relation to the Abrahamic sacrifice, those involved will be offered an "escape" from it if they so desire.

Polygamy is such a tough topic. It's tough for anyone that truly seeks to understand it. We may not ever fully understand it in this life, but hopefully some of the things in this chapter help people to look at this topic in a different light.

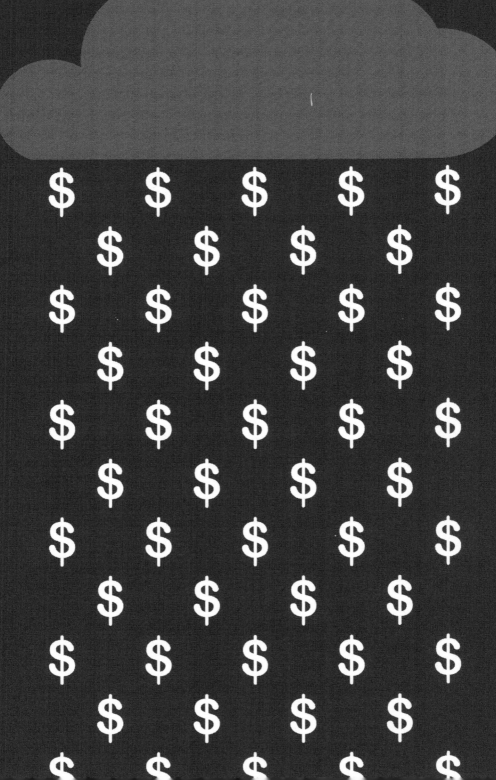

Looking at Tithing a Little Differently

If you've been going to church long enough, you have surely heard someone tell a variation of a story about how just after they paid their tithing, there appeared an extra five hundred bucks in their back pocket. In many of these and similar stories, the person telling the story feels that they were being rewarded financially because of their obedience to the law of tithing.

If you haven't heard that type of story, then maybe you've sat with a wealthy member of the Church and listened as they've attributed their good fortune to their diligence in paying a consistent tithe throughout their life. Provided they made their wealth legitimately, then who can find fault with them for wanting to humbly ascribe their wealth to keeping the commandments? Why wouldn't God want to bless someone who willfully and graciously pays an honest tithe?

I mean, it's right there in the scriptures over and over again, right? "Inasmuch as ye shall keep the commandments, ye shall prosper in the land" (Alma 9:13—and almost every other chapter in the Book of Mormon).

So . . . I've been thrown into a couple of different quandaries:

1. What about Brother So-and-so's family, who have faithfully paid their tithing for many, many years, and yet they can't ever seem to ever get ahead in life? They've "done everything right" and yet they struggle constantly . . . and have almost nothing.

2. What about the many people who choose not to pay their tithing, yet they still seem to be able to make insane amounts of money?

Almost every time we hear a talk in Church about tithing, someone will cite the scripture in Malachi that says, "Prove me now herewith, saith the Lord of hosts, if I will not open you the windows of heaven, and pour you out a blessing, that there shall not be room enough to receive it" (Malachi 3:10).

Sometimes I think we hear that scripture coupled with others stories, and we might wonder, "Well, I pay my tithing . . . so why don't those financial blessings happen to me? Where are my overflowing blessings? Am I paying my tithing wrong?"

The rest of that scripture in Malachi goes like this: "And I will rebuke the devourer for your sakes, and he shall not destroy the fruits of your ground; neither shall your vine cast her fruit before the time in the field, saith the Lord of hosts" (Malachi 3:11).

So what we're looking at are two types of blessings. The first and most appealing blessing is the promise of the windows of heaven pouring down upon us. Left to our carnal imaginations, we tend to associate this first blessing with unending temporal wealth and financial security. The second blessing, regarding the "fruit of your ground," is basically saying that you will have food on the table.

Nowhere in any scripture does it say that we'll be made temporally rich because we paid our tithing. No prophet or apostle that I am aware of has guaranteed that. In fact, over the course of scriptural history, prophets that have consecrated all that they had remained poor because of their commitment to the gospel.

Check out what the Lord says to Joseph Smith: "For thou shalt devote all thy service in Zion; and in this thou shalt have strength" (D&C 24:7). Joseph is probably thinking, "Ummm . . . so what does that mean?" And in the very next verse, the Lord says, "Be patient in afflictions, for thou shalt have many."

And now Joseph is probably thinking, "Sweet . . . but I'm still not sure where this is going."

Then the Lord gets even more specific: "In temporal labors thou shalt not have strength, for this is not thy calling." Meaning, you might be completely obedient to the commandments yet still remain poor.

It's not accurate to assume that someone's wealth came as a result of excessive righteousness. The most righteous and faithful individual could struggle financially all their life, while a lukewarm, inconsistent fence-sitter might acquire wealth without breaking a sweat.

So regardless of where I've been at financially in my life, I have always looked at paying tithing a little differently. I can't help but look at myself as a shareholder in God's kingdom. I think anyone who contributes to this kingdom can be considered a shareholder in that kingdom. I look at tithing as a short- and long-term investment. Short-term because I physically see temples and churches being built around the globe. Long-term because I know that according to Paul, God wants us to be "heirs," inheritors and possessors of all that He has (Romans 8:17). I feel ownership over every asset that the Church owns. I'm part of it and it is part of me. I feel like that is how God wants me to feel. Every time I enter a temple, I can honestly say that I've made an investment in it, however small it may be.

I don't think it's blasphemous to think this way. It makes total sense to me. Think about it. God doesn't need us to build temples, build churches, or even pay tithing. He could do it all himself. If He can assemble an earth, then He'll have no problem assembling a temple. So why does He have us do it? Why does He watch the Saints in their poverty build the Salt Lake temple for forty years when He could have done it much faster? Why does He ask you or I to pay tithing? Why are we asked to serve in so many ways when He could just do it all?

Because these temples, these meetinghouses, these sacrifices are not ultimately for Him. They're for us. God doesn't need these things. We do. And He wants us to be invested in the process of exaltation. He wants to know if we're willing to do what it takes to become like Him—and when we've proven ourselves, He gives us a return on our investment beyond our imaginations. "Eye hath not seen, nor ear heard, neither have entered into the heart of man, the things which God hath prepared for them that love him" (1 Corinthians 2:9).

How do we show Him that we love Him? How does anyone show anyone that they love something? It has everything to do with investment. In almost every case that I can think of, a person invests the most in the people and things they love the most.

When I look at tithing through this point of view, it makes me appreciate the opportunity that I have to contribute and invest in something worthwhile. Many may look at it merely as an act of obedience, and there is truth to that. But obedience, coupled with perspective and understanding, is much more powerful and exciting.

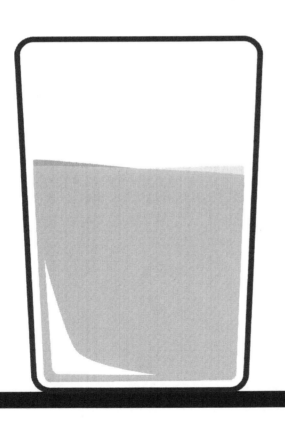

A Cool Glass of Water on a Sunday

People are beginning to see the Sabbath for what it is. Let me explain:

Have you ever looked forward to a general conference because you were certain in your mind that the apostles were going to address some of the crazy issues that are taking place in the world? "There's got to be some big announcement this time," we might say. "Maybe this is the year we'll be asked to 'flee to Zion,'" you might think. But then they talk about something like "Sabbath day observance" and we tune out because "we've heard this all before," right?

In recent times, the world seems to be crumbling in every way imaginable—yet all we seem to hear about is the Sabbath? I've been curious to know why.

As the Sabbath has been talked about with greater intensity, I've noticed quite a few people online say that they're sick of hearing about it. For me personally, it's generally the things I'm not doing so well with that I get sick of hearing about. "The guilty taketh the truth to be hard, for it cutteth them to the very center" (1 Nephi 16:2). I've been there . . . especially when it comes to the Sabbath.

The other reason people might get sick of hearing about the Sabbath is because of a lack of understanding. With that lack of understanding comes an associated lack of importance. When we don't understand something, we tend to think of it as not being very important. If a person doesn't truly understand the "why" of the Sabbath, then it just becomes a day of guilt, confusion, and boredom.

It's hard for the Sabbath day to become a "delight" when you never know if what you're doing is right. (Did you like that rhyme?)

When I hear someone give their Sabbath Kumbaya stories about how everyone sits in a circle on Sunday and reads scriptures all day after singing hymns together, sometimes it feels hard to measure up. Honestly, it just doesn't seem like reality.

Maybe I'm weird, and my thinking was off, but over the years, I've felt like all I could do on the Sabbath was eat, drink, sleep, read scriptures, pray, and go to church. This was because I was supposed to be "resting" from my labors and making the day "holy."

It also seemed to me like most people's Sabbath-day activities mainly involved sleeping or napping after church. But I hate sleeping during the day, so that just doesn't work for me. If I sleep all day Sunday, I feel horrible. It ruins my sleep pattern, and I can't go to sleep Sunday night, making Monday morning dreadful and setting me up for a brutal work week. I feel much better if I go for a walk or a hike outside or something else that involves nature.

But am I breaking the Sabbath?

Am I making the day less holy by taking a hike instead of being conked out on the couch all day, "resting"? Some might say that I am.

For me personally, I've spent many a Sunday after church in my parents' backyard, shooting baskets with my dad before dinner with the family. My mom would come outside and talk some trash to my dad when he missed his shots or just to jump into the conversation. It was so much fun, and I always looked forward to those times. We played horse or around the world or just stood there, holding the ball under our arms for hours. We'd sit as a family in our backyard chairs, talking about things we never had time to talk about during the week. During the week, we were too busy with our own things. My parents were working, I was playing on multiple sports teams and hanging out with friends. Honestly, I felt like the work week separated us. Every day took us further away from each other. The Sabbath brought us back together. And it was "delightful," if done in the right spirit.

This may seem sacrilegious to ask, but would I be a better person today or have a better relationship with my mom or dad if they left me by myself and were inside on the recliner, sleeping or reading their scriptures all day? I mean, no one would ever fault them for reading scriptures all day, would they? But surely people would fault them for bouncing that ball or firing up the BBQ outside . . . while not in their church clothes.

Fast forward twenty years: I have kids of my own who are shaping their perceptions of the Sabbath.

But is it all right to have fun on the Sabbath?

After church a few Sundays ago, it was beautiful outside. We got home from church at about noon and my kids begged me to go out back on the trampoline with them. Should I have said no?

Instead of saying no, I said, "Let's do it," and we spent the next ten minutes bouncing around on the trampoline. Rarely do I actually get the opportunity to do this. After I was too tired to bounce anymore, I laid on my back and looked up at the sky. Within two seconds, both kids were lying next to me, each placing their head on my left and right shoulders. They also stared up at the sky. In that moment, I was in their element, and they opened up to me. I was able to teach them and talk to them and strengthen them more so than I would have been able to in any other setting. I could have told them to go to their rooms and sleep. I could have told them to go read scriptures. I could have told them to go stare at the wall and be quiet because it's Sunday. But seriously?

I'm certain that there was no better thing I could have been doing with my Sabbath at that time. I could have been upstairs, writing church blogs or reading scriptures, and no man would condemn me. But I know that if I would have been doing anything else at that exact moment, I would have been condemning myself and ruining the most effective opportunity for me to bond with and strengthen my family.

This may sound crazy, but I truly believe that I would be breaking the Sabbath if all I did was read scriptures all day after church. Anyone who knows me well knows that it would be a dream for me to barricade myself in a room and read scriptures all day. I'm that nerdy. But if I did that, I seriously believe that I would be dishonoring the purpose of the Sabbath.

Again, no one would argue with someone for reading the scriptures or "taking a nap" on the Sabbath, but there are certainly some who would confidently suggest that we were breaking the Sabbath with every bounce of that trampoline.

So again, is it all right to have fun on the Sabbath?

According to both Elder Cook and Elder Bednar, of course it is.

Does that mean we should do whatever we want as long as we're "with our family?" No.

Recently we had to create another Sabbath tradition in our family. We decided, together, that we aren't going to play individual or team sports in our family on Sunday. My son was only seven at the time, and he made his little baseball all-star team. We were told that half of the games would be on Sunday. These games would cause us to miss church and by association, miss the sacrament. We'd also be required to be apart from each other for a good part of the day because of conflicting schedules.

Were we going to do doubleheaders on Sunday every time he made an all-star team or for travel ball? Would my son and I go to the games while my wife and daughter went to church because of a Relief Society responsibility? Would I shirk my callings to go to the Sunday games? Would my daughter, who loves sports, also start having Sunday conflicts? If one child was giving a talk in church, who would go watch the game and who would stay and watch the talk? Or would we just refuse the speaking opportunity altogether? We tracked the implications to what we considered to be a bad place for us, and from there, we made a tradition.

We weighed the arguments we'd hear against the tradition that we established.

"You're letting down the team."

"You made a commitment to the team," etc.

We came to the conclusion that one, it's just a game, and two, we made a commitment to God first. There was no way to satisfy both commitments without one or the other suffering. For us, there was no way to commit fully to both, and if we were going to be letting anyone down, it was going to be the team—not God. It needed to pass our Sabbath day "God and family first" litmus test. So from there, our traditions set a precedent for the future.

The cool thing is that this "no organized sports" tradition doesn't bother our kids because they look forward to the other traditions that make the Sabbath so enjoyable. In fact, they helped make the tradition. So now they're invested.

As far as I know, the Church has never—and I believe, never will—come out with a definitive list of what is and is not considered "keeping the Sabbath day holy."

I don't know if everything we do on Sunday (our traditions) are right or wrong, but what I do know is that our Sundays are set apart for God and family. That day is sacred to us. We all know that. We all feel that. We all look forward to it. It's a day in which our family comes closer and becomes stronger. It's also a day in which we bless other families through our callings.

Isn't it funny how everyone has their own perceptions of what is and is not allowed? I've had this discussion with countless people over the years, and I don't know of one family that does Sunday the same. Some think it's perfectly fine to come home after church and sleep all day but condemn the person who takes their family on a Sunday hike.

There are those who stay in their church clothes all day as a way of keeping the day holy. Others run home and throw on sweatpants and feel just as holy. Some think the Crock-Pot should be prepared on Saturday night so that they don't cook on Sunday. Others like to fire up the BBQ and pitch in together to make a meal on the Sabbath. Listing the various preferences could take us all night . . .

My point is that none of that is doctrine. None of it is even policy. Like the Pharisees of the past, we're so concerned with honoring our self-conceived lists that we forget to honor the Sabbath and enjoy it for what it is. To watch people argue about why their way of keeping the Sabbath is right while condemning others is quite the sight to see.

Elder Christofferson said that instead of focusing on what we can and cannot do, that we should be focusing on outcomes.[65]

So what's the desired outcome of the Sabbath day?

Is it to rest?

That depends on our definition of "rest." Did God rest from His labors on the Sabbath day because He was tired? Does anyone really believe that when God rested from His labors on the seventh day, that He went and found a cloudy recliner to isolate Himself for the afternoon?

In Genesis 2, when it says that God "rested" from His labors, the Hebrew lexicon defines "rest" as something very different from what we think of in English. Two Hebrew definitions stuck out to me:

1. "To repose" (which we usually associate with "peace" and "tranquility")
2. "To celebrate"[66]

Nowhere in the various contexts and definitions of the Sabbath have I found the concept of sleeping to be what the Lord intended us to do with that day. In fact, it seems to be quite the opposite.

---

65 D. Todd Christofferson in "Video: The Sabbath as a Delight," *October 2015: Sabbath Day Observance*, https://www.lds.org/broadcasts/archive/general-conference-leadership-training/2015/10?lang=eng.
66 Kairos Software, LLC. "Strong's Concordance KJV Bible." Apple App Store, Vers. 3.3.4 (2017). https://itunes.apple.com/us/app/strongs-concordance-kjv-bible/id1113008391?mt=8 (accessed on 28 September 2017).

When I was a missionary, Sundays were always my busiest days. Ward council in the morning, then off to make sure investigators made it to church all right. Then we'd stay close to those investigators and worry about making sure they had a good time. We'd make sure they got home safely and then go find people to teach. Then we'd have baptismal services, which we were often solely responsible for. Anyone who's been there and done that knows what I'm talking about. When you hit the pillow on Sunday night . . . you're whooped.

Talk to a mother or visit your local stake presidency or bishopric and ask them if they're tired at the end of the day. They're beat!

That doesn't seem like resting, now does it?

Unless . . . we define rest as it was originally given in the Hebrew. Even though I was tired on Sunday night after a busy day of missionary "work," there was never a time in my life that I experienced more "peace" and "tranquility." There was never a time in which I felt a greater desire to "celebrate" than at the end of those busy Sundays. I'm certain many others have felt the same way.

In a recent training on the Sabbath day, Sister Linda K. Burton talked about a tradition that began in her home with three teenage daughters. She talked about how it became a tradition for them to come together and make cookies and then deliver those cookies to people whom they thought might need them.[67] Now, you can just imagine three teenage daughters and a mom in the kitchen making cookies. It's a lot of work, and it probably makes a big mess to clean up. It's not what someone might consider "resting." Some may contend that they were breaking the Sabbath, and if they were making cookies to sell for money or for self-indulgence, I might agree. But they were making those cookies to bless and strengthen their "family," the fatherless and the widows and others who might need strengthening on a day that was set apart specifically for that kind of activity.

It's interesting. The same physical activity of making cookies can yield different Sabbath day outcomes.

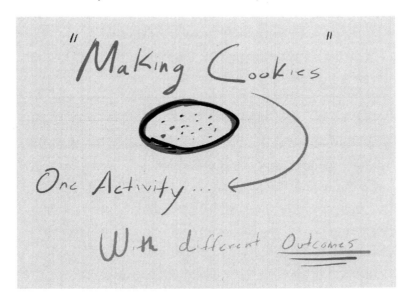

---

67 Linda K. Burton in "Video: The Sabbath as a Delight," *October 2015: Sabbath Day Observance*, https://www.lds.org/broadcasts/archive/general-conference-leadership-training/2015/10?lang=eng.

Some people say we should "give the Sabbath day back to the Lord." But I think that the Lord would give it right back to us and say, "The Sabbath was made for you . . . not you for the Sabbath" (Mark 2:27). In commenting on that scripture in Mark, Elder Nelson said, "I believe He [God] wanted us to understand that the Sabbath was His gift to us."[68]

Isaiah said that the Sabbath should be a delight (Isaiah 58:13). Not a party, but a delight. Make cookies for each other, have dinner together, sing songs together, mix in some scriptures, have fun, recharge!

The Sabbath day conversation is interesting because you think to yourself, "It's just a day of the week . . . what's the big deal? Why is it one of the big Ten Commandments? Why do modern apostles focus on this seemingly ancillary commandment?"

My personal belief is this: I believe the primary purpose of the Sabbath is to preserve the "religion of our families." The word "religion" comes from the Latin *religare*, which means "to bind." The Sabbath has always been thought of as the day in which we "get religion"—but if we take the true meaning of religion as our guide, the Sabbath is actually a day set apart for us "to bind" ourselves to our families.

---

68 Russell M. Nelson, "The Sabbath Is a Delight," *Ensign*, May 2015.

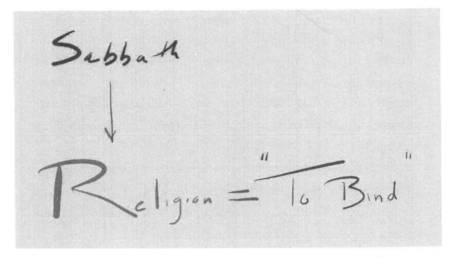

So the apostles might go to the Lord and ask, "What is the most important thing we should be focusing on?" If I had to guess the answer to that question, I believe it would have something to do with preserving families from this final onslaught of the last days.

"So what is the best way to go about preserving and protecting families?"

"Bind yourselves together on the Sabbath! That is why it was made!"

So when Elder Christofferson says that we should focus on outcomes, in my mind, the most desirable outcome for the Sabbath is that we would come together and bind ourselves back to each other with Christ's Atonement at the center of those activities. The at-one-ment is the ultimate reconciliation, binding, and sealing agent. It is at the heart of pure religion.

Pure religion, as James defines it, is to "visit the fatherless and the widows" and to "keep [yourself] unspotted from the world" (James 1:27).

Why the fatherless and the widows? Because they lack family members to bind (*religare*) with and derive strength from. That is why we come together on Sunday. To be with and strengthen both our immediate and ward families.

How do we keep ourselves unspotted from the world? "And that thou mayest more fully keep thyself unspotted from the world, thou shalt go to the house of prayer and offer up thy sacraments upon my holy day," Sunday (D&C 59:9).

Pure religion then, is the act of preserving families through the application of the Atonement of Christ. Almost all of this takes place on Sunday for us.

Each major Sabbath has been an act of grace worth celebrating. The creation of the earth, the Exodus (God's deliverance of His people out of bondage in Egypt), the Resurrection of Jesus Christ—all of these events revolved around one concept. That concept dealt with the deliverance, preservation, and progression of God's covenant families, and that is a concept worth celebrating!

The Sabbath has been something that has nagged at me for many years. It's always bugged me because I never had a hard and fast rule to determine whether what I was doing on the Sabbath was right or wrong. But I've finally come up with a rule that brings peace to my mind for any and every Sabbath activity.

My Sabbath Rule:

Always make sacrifices that strengthen your relationship with God and with family. You know you're violating the Sabbath if you are making sacrifices that weaken those relationships.

Easy.

When I apply that rule to each Sabbath activity, I find peace, tranquility, and a cause to celebrate. To paraphrase Elder Bednar, the Sabbath becomes like a cool drink of water after a hot day of working in the sun.[69]

Happy Sabbath to you all!

---

69 David A. Bednar in "Video: The Sabbath as a Delight," *October 2015: Sabbath Day Observance*, https://www.lds.org/broadcasts/archive/general-conference-leadership-training/2015/10?lang=eng.

The Place for Gays inside the Church

Not too long ago, I flew to Boston to speak at a public affairs conference. When I finished speaking, I had the opportunity to shake hands and mingle with the great people who had attended. As I was getting ready to leave, a man came up to me in the foyer, shook my hand, and introduced himself as a gay man. I told him it was so great to meet him and he proceeded to tell me a bit about his background. I didn't say much because I know that this can be a sensitive topic for many people, and so he did a great deal of the talking. I just wanted to keep my mouth shut and listen to this brother's story.

We hear a lot about people who have been raised in the Church but who subsequently "came out of the closet" and are trying to deal with the associated familial, social, and ecclesiastical pressures of being gay. But this man's story was very different. I listened intently as he explained to me that he did not grow up in the Church. He told me that he was a convert to the Church in one of the most liberal college towns in the United States: Cambridge, Massachusetts. I was sort of shocked, to be honest. With all that is going on with social media, a gay Mormon convert seemed like last person I'd run into while speaking in Cambridge. I'm sure he could read the surprise on my face as he began to tell his story. We joked about how much of an enigma he is inside the Church. A gay man . . . converting to Mormonism?! How?! But what he told me next . . . I'll never forget.

This good, kind man said this:

> I believe that there is a place for gays inside of the Mormon Church. The doctrine of the Church tells me that I have a place here. Nothing I have learned inside the Church tells me that I don't have a place here. It is the media and those who are critical to the Church that persistently tell me that I don't have a place here, but the doctrine tells me otherwise.

When I heard this, I just stood there. I felt the Spirit so strongly, standing there in that foyer with this brother. This gay Mormon man—a recent convert—just spoke the truth, and the Spirit testified of it to me. People with homosexual feelings need to know that they absolutely have a place in the Church. They should have a place among us just as much as anyone else. Members of the Church need to know this. Critics need to know this. And the world needs to know that prophets and apostles continue to back it up, even from the pulpit in general conference. "We cannot," as Elder Ballard said, "stand on the sidelines while others, including our critics, attempt to define what the Church teaches."[70] The Church teaches inclusion. It is at the core of our doctrine. If a member of the Church is discriminating, it doesn't mean that the Church is discriminating.

Look, I can't understand homosexuality. I just can't. As a man who loves his wife and is so naturally and physically attracted to her, I can't wrap my head around it. Personally, to feel that way toward another man just doesn't register in my brain. But that doesn't mean I can't be understanding to another man who feels differently. There's nothing he or anyone else can do about the way he feels toward men, in just the same way that there is never a chance that anyone could change the natural desire I have for my wife. But for a gay man or woman, who can't help the way he or she feels, it can be a scary, lonely, and confusing predicament to be in when it comes to having a desire to follow biblical Christianity.

The official stance of the Church is simply this: "God loves all of us. He loves those of different faiths and those without any faith. He loves those who suffer. He loves the rich and poor alike. He loves people of every race and culture, the married or single, and those who experience same-sex attraction or identify as gay, lesbian, or bisexual. And God expects us to follow His example."[71]

---

70 M. Russell Ballard, "Using New Media to Support the Work of the Church," Brigham Young University–Hawaii commencement address, Dec. 15, 2007; devotional.byuh.edu.
71 "Church Teachings," MormonandGay.LDS.org, accessed September 28, 2017, https://mormonandgay.lds.org/articles/church-teachings.

I love that.

"And God expects us to follow His example."

We don't follow His example by ensuring that we're on the clear other side of the chapel from that gay member or by talking behind his back. We follow His example by pulling up a seat right next to him and figuring out how to be his friend. We follow God's example by not treating that person differently than we might treat others. We follow God's example by being "no respecter of persons." We follow God's example by recognizing that each of us has challenges and each of us has sinned.

But keep in mind that just because a man or woman is attracted to the same sex, it doesn't mean they're sinning. Elder Ballard said, "Let us be clear: The Church of Jesus Christ of Latter-day Saints believes that 'the experience of same–sex attraction is a complex reality for many people. The attraction itself is not a sin, but acting on it is. Even though individuals do not choose to have such attractions, they do choose how to respond to them.' "[72]

It has never been my job in life to determine where someone else's testosterone or estrogen levels fall within the Kinsey scale. I don't know if a person is gay because they were born that way or whether it was because of social circles, friends, or the confusing world we live in. I believe there are some of both. But truly, I don't know why anyone is the way that they are—and again, it's not my job to figure

---

72 M. Russell Ballard, "Be Still, and Know that I am God,"
Church Educational System Devotional for young adults, May 4, 2014.

it out. It's not my job to speculate or keep track of whether or not my brother or sister is sinning in a homosexual or a heterosexual way. As long as what others are doing doesn't affect me directly, it's really none of my business. My business is to live according to the light and knowledge that I have. My business is to follow Christ's example and love my brothers and sisters. Plain and simple. The rest is up to God alone.

God is not going to distinguish between homosexual and heterosexual sin. Even the least sin will keep each us from entering the kingdom of God without faith in Christ, repentance, and personal and spiritual growth. Sexual sin is forbidden, regardless of whether or not you're gay or straight. The Bible forbids it on each end of the spectrum. God forbids men being with women outside of marriage and He forbids men being with men outside of marriage. But He also states that marriage is between a man and a woman, which is much more difficult for someone who truly has been dealt the hand of homosexuality. That is all the more reason for us to rally around someone who is trying to deal with that circumstance in his or her life. Alma describes Christ as one who "will take upon him their infirmities, that his bowels may be filled with mercy, according to the flesh, that he may know according to the flesh how to succor his people according to their infirmities" (Alma 7:12). Christ shows empathy towards each of us. His bowels are filled with mercy toward *everyone*—those who are working through challenging times in their lives.

This brother I met in Boston was completely right. The doctrine of Christ testifies that there is a place for him in the Church . . . and it's right next to me on the pew.

Don't Take Advantage of Members

"You never check your religion at the door."
—Jeffrey R. Holland[73]

O ver the years I've had the great opportunity to do business with a lot of good members of the Church. For the most part, I've loved doing business with these people. They are generally honest and upright. Kind and reasonable. Patient and understanding. I've always felt like I knew where they were coming from, and that regardless of any quirks they had, I still felt like they were good people at their core.

But once in a great while you come across a bad apple. Their logic is flawed, and they reek of contradictions. These types of people sometimes appear to be the cream of the

---

73 Jeffrey R. Holland, "Israel, Israel, God Is Calling," Church Educational System Devotional for young adults, January 2012, https://www.lds.org/broadcasts/article/ces-devotionals/2012/01/israel-israel-god-is-calling?lang=eng.

crop. Often they're successful, and money is not an object. Each of them appears to be quite dedicated and engaged in their Church service and callings. I've observed them to actually be quite giving when it comes to their faith and helping others at church.

But then one day you have a conversation with one of these people about their philosophy on business, life, the Church, and their compartmentalization of each of them. A few of these conversations have left me dumbfounded and confused.

"It's just business," they'd say as they explain why they acted in such and such a way during this or that business transaction.

This one little phrase is the most hypocritical thing a Christian business person can ever say: "It's just business!" As if that is supposed to somehow excuse them from observing the tenants of their faith when money is involved. I have listened to those whom I've considered to be good people explain that they are very careful to "separate business from religion." They've explained that in business, they may need to do things that they are not necessarily proud of. Some are very upfront about this fact, and I sit there trying to make sense of that logic. Many of them will justify questionable "business practices" in the name of their family. They'll contest that they've "got a family to feed" and are therefore required to make sacrifices, even if those sacrifices betray their core beliefs.

Never should a business come before the God who gave you that business.

In my mind, it's not possible to separate your business from your religion. To quote Jeffrey R. Holland, there is no possible reason that you should ever "check your religion at the door." The way you run or manage a business should reflect the teachings and leadership of Christ. The way you treat people inside and outside of your organization should not make their professional lives miserable. Quite the contrary! You should strive to make the business environment safe, secure, and enjoyable. It is, after all, many people's "home away from home"!

But too many Christian business owners are out there trying to grind people, sue people, and exercise dominion over people. The mentality of this type of person is one that must win *at everything*. It's not enough to do a fair deal. They need it to be the best deal for them and a bad deal for the other parties involved. They seek to exploit others in their weakness in order to extract a maximum profit on the deal.

But "it's just business," right?

Their actions are subtly saying, "Nevertheless, fear God—he will justify in committing a little sin; yea, lie a little, take the advantage of one because of his words, dig a pit for thy neighbor; there is no harm in this; and do all these things, for tomorrow we die; and if it so be that we are guilty, God will beat us with a few stripes, **and at last we shall be saved in the kingdom of God**" (2 Nephi 28:8; emphasis added).

It doesn't at all work that way.

Calling someone a "shrewd businessman" used to be an insult. Now it seems fashionable. But you don't have to be shrewd to make money. I would rather live a life of making fair deals in which both parties involved feel good about the deal than be 20% richer when I'm 65 years old. If I'm going to give my family something when I die, I'd much rather it be a legacy of integrity than an extra million bucks. That kind of legacy is one that will never rust or burn or diminish with time.

After all, as the once-successful Job stated, "Naked came I out of my mother's womb, and naked shall I return thither: the Lord gave, and the Lord hath taken away" (Job 1:21). As my mission president used to say, "You'll never see a hearse towing a U-Haul to the cemetery."

It should never only be "just business." It should be about people and the impact you can have on them. In studies of effective business leaders these days, there is a popular trend toward "servant-based leadership" among the most effective leaders. Go figure. Christ was teaching that almost 2,000 years ago. It was then, and is now, the most effective way to lead and manage a business or transaction.

Making a living occupies so much of our lives. Therefore, the way in which we make that living is one of the most significant determinants of our character. Our character is what we give to our families, and our character is what we take back to God.

It's never "just business."

On the other hand, there are some people who want you to do everything for them for free because they're in your ward or are members. We ain't living the law of consecration yet . . . so pay up.

I Really Do Believe

"Shall we not go on in so great a cause?"
—Joseph Smith (D&C 128:22)

Endure ridicule, no matter what they say. There is a sifting taking place in the Church that will require you to lean on logical belief and the ratifying comfort and confirmation of those beliefs through the Holy Ghost.

Over the last few years I've been making an effort to share my testimony of the gospel online. But I never could have imagined the things people would say about me for doing so. I mean, I grew up in California in a place where there weren't a ton of Mormons. Most of my friends weren't members of the Church, so I was made fun of—though none of it was ever hostile. Just friends doing what friends do to any Mormon who's outnumbered 20 to 1 in a baseball dugout. It's all good. :)

But as I've published a few blogs over the last couple years now, I've been dumbfounded by the number of people who have relentlessly made fun of me and my testimony in the most callous ways. It was hard at first to read the comments and messages, but in time, it taught me a huge lesson. So, to anyone who has made fun of me for "staying in Mormonism," I want to tell you what's in my heart regarding the Church and its validity.

I want you to know that I'm just a normal guy that wants to do the right thing in life. I'm constantly and honestly trying to learn, research, and grow. I'm not being "willfully blind" to the truth and thereby abiding in a lie because I have nothing better to do. I have no interest in living a lie or dedicating my life to a fraud. I have no desire to get up at 4:30 a.m. to teach a seminary class or to work an early morning temple shift if everything I believe about the Restoration is made up. I have no desire to give up ten percent of my income for nothing and no desire to give up my Sundays for no good reason. I have nothing to gain temporally by staying in the Church.

When I left on my mission, I also had nothing temporal to gain by leaving. I was already 21 years old, and I had a full scholarship to play baseball in Hawaii, interest from a couple major league baseball scouts, a fiancée, lots of friends, and surfboards—and my parents never pressured me to go. No one came up to me when I was 21 and in college and said, "Hey, I'm gonna bring you in on this fraud, and I want you to give up everything you're doing to go around and lie to people—and oh, by the way, you'll get nothing for it in return." Do you realize how fast my 21-year-old self would have told the dude to "get lost," had that been the case?

My point is that there is absolutely no good or logical reason why I would leave on a mission and continue as a member of this Church unless I honestly believed it was true and good.

So when someone writes to me (which is quite often) and tells me that they know that *I* know that I am lying and purposely trying to lead people astray by giving my own personal testimony about what I believe regarding the truthfulness of the Church, my only question is WHY? Why would I do such a thing if I didn't honestly believe it was true? What is the gain? The motivation? Even just one valid reason?

No one paid me to serve a mission. I didn't get any kind of temporal reward for those two years or any of the subsequent ten years of Church service. There was no conflict of interest. No secret plan.

When I returned home from my mission, I've had no reason to lie and say that I loved my mission or that it was a defining moment in my life. It makes me sad when people who don't even know me tell me that I'm lying about my beliefs. Again . . . why would I? Why waste the time and energy? I have no ulterior motives for staying in the Church other than the fact that I believe in it. I truly believe in it. If I didn't believe it was true, then I would chalk it up as just another man made institution and be on my way. Are you kidding? If I thought it was a fraud, I wouldn't waste another moment of my life thinking about it.

But for me personally, I truly have nowhere else to go. I've incessantly studied other religions and philosophies for years. I've looked deeply at agnosticism and atheism and tried to find some semblance of logic in them. I've studied every ounce of literature I could get my hands on that is critical to the Mormon faith. And still, the validity of the Church is logical to me. I've searched high and low and haven't come across anything better. Like Peter said, "To whom shall [I] go?" (John 6:68). Absolutely nothing I've studied satisfies my innate deepest desires and hopes the way that Mormon doctrine does. That has been my experience. I can't argue or dispute what I've felt and heard.

Everybody believes something. If I was to read a blog of someone's testimony of Lutheranism, Agnosticism, or Wiccan, I would have absolutely no desire to write mean things about that person. I might disagree with the things written, possibly consider it misguided, or just pass it by for being so ludicrous as to not be worth my time . . . but never would I imagine spending so much time trying to prove that person wrong. I don't dislike that person just because I don't agree with their beliefs about God. At the end of the day, regardless of a person's belief, love is always better than hate. Positivity and respect is always better than negativity and disdain.

It seems as if so many people want to control the thoughts, actions, and beliefs of others. Some people make fun of me by calling me a "TBM" or "True Believing Mormon," and then I'll read one of their comments in which they admit to being a "TBM" only a year or so ago. They'll get mad at me for being a "TBM" just because I didn't have the same negative experience that they had that caused them to stop believing in the Church. They want to ridicule me into not believing anymore just because they've stopped believing. And if I don't listen to them right then and there, I'm accused of perpetuating and covering up a lie, as if I'm privy to some kind of underground information. It's what atheists have done to believers for ages. "I've stopped believing—and now you must do the same . . . or you're an idiot."

But here's what I can't understand. Why would anyone on earth spend their time thinking and worrying about the Church if they don't believe it's true? If it is indeed a fraud, and you have already moved on, saved 10% of your income, freed up loads of time, and broken free from the "shackles of Mormonism," then what motivates you to ever read one of my ignorant blog posts, discuss it on Reddit with the basest of language, write apologetics, or create video rebuttals or entire podcast series against what I've written or what FAIR's written or any number of LDS writers have written? I like my belief. It makes me better, plain and simple. That fact only helps me to treat others better, which is an overall micro-benefit for humanity.

There are a lot of people who will concur with the fact that being a member of the Church makes them happy. Many of those same people are they who know what it's like to not have the Church in their life. They've seen the contrast and can attest to the stark differences. That is real. It's not hype. It's not made up. There is no other motivation other than following what they've felt in their hearts.

I understand that everyone is not the same. I have plenty of friends and family members who have chosen a direction and belief system that is completely contrary to everything that I believe. But I have no desire to argue with them or criticize them for the path that they have chosen. I just love them and am grateful for our friendship. So you can make fun of me for being a Mormon, but please just realize this one thing: I absolutely believe it is true. With all my heart, I believe that it is true.

What's Not to Love?

For all that might be said about Mormon culture and its associated foibles and weaknesses, there is one thing that I will always love about "those Mormons." This attribute that I love so much is something that has gotten them, as a people, through some of the most troubling times any group of people has ever faced. It's gotten them through a time in which they were the only people in the land to have an extermination order out against them. During the history of this world, we've seen horrible periods of slavery. We've seen people's lands taken from them. We've seen prejudice and discrimination. But it's a rare occasion in which a group of people are sought after for complete annihilation. To extinguish them from the land because of a belief. Well, not quite. It was a little more than that. Persecutors of the Church in the early days saw how loyal the members of the

Church were to each other. They saw how they moved as one and how powerful they were as they did so. That was scary to many of the people in those frontier towns from an economic and political point of view. It was as if the Mormons were one giant family, one heart and one mind, regardless of their individual differences.

Because of all this history, Mormons had to learn to stick together, take care of their own, and have each other's back. That's why when a person joins this Church, they are literally gaining a family—and it is truly like a family. As I grew up in my own biological family, I had one sister. We loved each other . . . but there was no end to the things we'd do to annoy each other. I would find ways to irritate, annoy, and bug her. She would tell my mom or dad. Then she might scratch or push me, whine or cry. I'd get in trouble for "doing nothing," as I always explained, and possibly get sent to my room. But through it all, I always had her back, and I will always have her back. I know that she has my back, and if I was in dire need of something, she'd drop everything, put her life on hold, and come to the rescue. There's a special bond that exists among family members. As my sister once told me, "Truly, you are the only one on this earth that knows why I am the way that I am."

In the Church, there might be some shoving, some bickering, some arguing, and maybe even some fighting. But at the end of the day, I'd be there for any of my brothers and sisters. I know them, and I know what's in their heart. That's the thing I love most about Mormons as a people. Regardless of what's going on, when people need help, they help. They set aside their differences and come together to provide strength for each other at just the right time. I can imagine the children of Israel, living through miserable conditions at the hands of their captors, making mistakes, and arguing with each other as they made their way out of Egypt, through Sinai, and eventually into their "promised land." I can see those early Christian Church members under Nero and the ten pagan persecutions, drawing fishes in the desert sand[74] as they were driven from place to place, left homeless and scared. I can see them arguing in the same way that Peter and Paul used to argue about this or that doctrine or historical event, but when the rubber met the road, they would come together in unity to support each other and support the cause.

Sometimes I think Mormons take what they have in each other for granted, in just the same way we take our own families for granted sometimes. That Christian fish that was drawn in the sand almost 2000 years ago by members of the Lord's Church was a desperate attempt to find and reunite with their brothers and sisters so that they could come together and draw strength from one another. We may not have ten Caesars coming after us with swords and armies at this time in our lives, but we have other threats that are just as dangerous to our progression in life. People may not like to go to meetings or give talks in church, but

---

74 See Elesha Coffman, "What is the origin of the Christian fish symbol?" *Christianity Today*, August 2008, http://www.christianitytoday.com/history/2008/august/what-is-origin-of-christian-fish-symbol.html.

I know that if I go down with a sickness, or need someone to talk to, or need some help in any way, there will be soft hearts and smiling faces coming out of the woodwork. That is something I know. That is something I can testify of, something I've experienced.

What I see is a church that is moving in the right direction. It's moving in the right direction as God inspires men and women to make corrections and improvements along the way. Why doesn't God just give us all the answers and make everything perfect for us? Because that is not how we'll learn. He wants us, as a people, to figure out how to work together and overcome obstacles. He's like a proud daddy who starts his child out on a bicycle with training wheels and watches them go. As the training wheels come off, he stands by closely, with his hands ready to catch us as we try to find our balance. Then he gives us a shove and lets us pedal away. If we forget to brake and we run into a tree, he runs over and picks us up. If we lose our balance on a bumpy road, fall down, and get some scrapes, he cleans us up and helps us get right back up.

I see good things from the Church. I see good things from the people. I see the culture changing for the better. I see mistakes being admitted and corrected. I see improvements everywhere. And I see the gospel of Jesus Christ in its fullness blessing the entire world.

About the Author

G reg Trimble is an Internet blogger who has reached millions of people around the world through his writings. He is the CEO of Yalla—an online team management and project collaboration application. He's also the founder of Lemonade Stand—a digital marketing agency located in Southern California.

Greg's articles have been picked up and syndicated by major news outlets around the country. He speaks nationally to various congregations about the power of the Internet and social media in sharing the gospel of The Church of

Jesus Christ of Latter-day Saints. He has a passion for the logic and beauty of the gospel and has taught as an institute and seminary teacher for six years.

Greg loves to surf, play golf, and, above all else, hang out with his wife, Kristyn, and his two kids, Taylor and Trenton."

Excerpt from Greg Trimble. *Dads Who Stay and Fight*. iBooks. https://itunes.apple.com/us/book/dads-who-stay-and-fight/id1223020703?mt=11

Made in the USA
San Bernardino, CA
20 August 2018